Alan Dunn's
Flowers and Foliage for
Wedding Cakes

Inspirational sugar sprays
for contemporary designs

For Kristofer, Grandma, Roux and Lizzi

Acknowledgements

A huge thank you to Beverley and Rob Dutton for commissioning the book that has taken almost forever for me to complete – none of us intended it to take this long! Many thanks to the team who have worked so hard in the production of this book – especially to Jenny Stewart for her editing skills, Sarah Richardson for the design of the book, Alister Thorpe for photography, and Robin Nattress for collecting the initial batch of cakes in the oversized white van! Thank you also to my friends Kristofer Kerrigan-Graham and Alice Kilgour-Christie for their invaluable help and support throughout the making of this book, particularly their help in making mistletoe! To Jaime and David Maccoy for allowing me to use their wedding cake in this book; to Jean and Steve Folan for accommodation in-between photoshoot days; to Myra and George Taylor for overnight accommodation, kindness and the orange dahlia; and to Tombi Peck for transporting me and the cakes to the final photoshoot and allowing me to change and use her fruitcake recipe in this book. Thank you to Renshaws for providing all the sugarpaste used in the book. Finally, thanks to my wonderful parents Allen and Avril for their love and support.

First published in March 2005 by B. Dutton Publishing Limited, Alfred House, Hones Business Park, Farnham, Surrey, GU9 8BB, UK.

Reprinted in August 2007.

Copyright: Alan Dunn 2005

ISBN 10: 1-905113-00-5

ISBN 13: 978-1-905113-00-2

Publisher: Beverley Dutton

Editor: Jenny Stewart

Design: Sarah Richardson

Editorial Assistant: Clare Porter

Design Assistant: Zena Manicom

Photography: Alister Thorpe

Printed in China by arrangement with Associated Agencies Ltd.

Introduction

Flowers and Foliage for Wedding Cakes is my eighth book. It began life as a rumour – I'm not quite sure where, or how it started, but I had a couple of phone calls from friends asking when my new book on exotic fruit and vegetables was due to be published. Whilst I was very puzzled and intrigued at first, I felt inspired to start writing another book. After a quick phone call to Beverley Dutton at B. Dutton Publishing with an explanation of events, a new book about sugar foliage was commissioned.

As you can see, that plan changed slightly. Having been informed by my previous publisher that my other books were out of print (or soon to be), the decision was made to broaden the theme and try to strike a happy balance between the flowers and foliage, adding the odd fruit and berry to the collection too. I was keen to feature many new subjects as well as some old favourites of mine, with the aim to include projects that would appeal to novice and experienced sugar flower makers alike, and also provide inspiration to future brides in choosing a wedding cake design for their special day.

Whilst there are instructions for decorating real cakes for each of the designs, I often prefer to use dummy cakes for the fully decorated wedding cake display, and to provide a simply iced cutting cake. One advantage is that you can cut the real cake in advance and wrap each slice in wax paper and then decorative tissue paper, providing a ready-wrapped gift for the wedding guests to take home after the event. There is also the issue of health and safety. Although sugar flowers are made from edible flower paste, they usually contain wires, stamens and floristry tape, none of which are intended for food use! Moreover, there are strict food laws governing what colours can be used on a cake, so whilst there is still a huge number of food colours available from sugarcraft specialists such as Squires Kitchen, many of the bright pinks, purples and blues that I love to use on my flowers are no longer deemed to be edible, and so are classified as craft dusts. There has been a revival recently in the use of fresh flowers on cakes too, but this is a tricky practice. Many flowers are poisonous to some degree, so are best avoided on real cakes. Using a polystyrene dummy cake means that I can use any of these mediums happily on the display cake knowing that it is not going to be eaten.

The flowers featured in this book have been made using sugar (flower paste) and another allied inedible medium, cold porcelain. Flower paste is a great medium to make flowers from – it can be rolled finely, frilled and formed to form quite realistic effects. However, it can be very fragile. Cold porcelain is completely inedible but is a much stronger material when dry. Whilst some sugar florists prefer not to use inedible pastes, I feel it helps to broaden my interest and develop skills that also help with my sugar flower making. The instructions in this book are given for sugar flower making, with some extra information about cold porcelain at the back of the book.

I hope you will enjoy trying out some of the flowers, foliage and wedding cakes in this book as much as I did when I made them. Try to invent your own combination of flowers to create an inspired style of your own.

Contents

Orchid and Lotus

Dendrobium Nobile orchids, carnations, green lotus pods and clary sage form an interesting collaboration on this single tiered cake. Extended curly lengths of purple paper-covered wire help to connect the flowers and cake together.

Cake and Decoration

25.5cm (10") teardrop shaped rich fruitcake

Apricot glaze

1kg (2lb) white almond paste

700g (1¹/₂lb) white sugarpaste mixed with 700g (1¹/₂lb) champagne sugarpaste

Clear alcohol (e.g. white rum, cherry or orange liqueur)

Fine lilac ribbon to trim the cake

Royal icing

Broad lime ribbon to trim the cake drum

Non-toxic glue stick

SK Cream Paste Food Colour

Equipment

35.5cm (14") oval cake drum

Piping bag

No. 0 piping tube

Candleholder

Purple paper-covered wire

Flowers and Foliage

Orchid and lotus spray
(see pages 18-19)

Preparation

1. Brush the teardrop shaped rich fruitcake with apricot glaze and cover with white almond paste. Use sugarpaste smoothers to achieve a good finish. Trim away the excess paste from the base. Allow to dry overnight.

2. Mix together the equal proportions of white and champagne sugarpaste. Moisten the surface of the almond paste with clear alcohol and cover the cake with sugarpaste. Use a pair of sugarpaste smoothers to achieve a smooth finish. Press a pad of sugarpaste into the palm of your hand and use this to smooth and polish the difficult curve of the cake. Cover the oval board with paste. Smooth and trim off the excess paste. Transfer the cake to the board and allow to dry.

3. Attach a fine band of lilac ribbon to the base of the cake, using a tiny amount of royal icing to secure it in place. Decorate the edge of the board with a length of pale lime ribbon and secure with non-toxic glue.

Side Design

4. Fit a piping bag with a No. 0 piping tube. Half-fill with cream coloured royal icing and pipe a series of dots and curls over the surface of the cake and the board.

Assembly

5. Wire the flowers together into a spray (see pages 18 to 19). Tie the spray onto the candleholder using some of the purple paper-covered wire. Position the arrangement behind the curve of the cake. Tease and curl the lengths of paper-covered wire over the cake to create an attractive finish.

Dendrobium Nobile Orchid

This widely distributed orchid can be found growing wild over vast areas of India, Thailand and Vietnam. There are many species and hybrid forms of this orchid with a colour range of white, yellow, pink and purple.

Materials

Holly/Ivy coloured and white flower paste

24 and 26-gauge white wires

Nile green and white floristry tape

African violet, aubergine and plum craft dusts

SK Edelweiss, Forest Green, Holly/Ivy, Leaf Green and Vine Dust Food Colours

SK Cyclamen Liquid Food Colour

Half-strength SK Confectioners' Glaze

Equipment

Ceramic silk veining tool (HP)

Dendrobium Montrose cutters: 846-848 (TT)

SK Great Impressions Amaryllis Petal Veiner (wide)

Metal ball tool (CC)

SK Great Impressions Stargazer B Petal Veiner

Fine paintbrush

Plain-edge cutting wheel (PME)

Column

1. This is the piece that contains the stamens of the flower and is used to support the throat petal. In this particular orchid it is quite short in length. Roll a ball of white flower paste and then form it into a teardrop shape. Hollow out the inside of the column by placing the teardrop alongside the rounded end of a ceramic tool; try to position it so that the rounded end of the teardrop is slightly above the tool. Carefully press the two together using your finger and thumb at the same time to create a ridge down the back of the column.

2. Form a small 'ski-stick' hook in the end of a 24-gauge wire. Moisten the hook and pull through the throat, about a third of the way down from the rounded tip of the column. The hook should be embedded into the paste. Add a tiny ball of paste over the hook to hide it.
Blend the paste onto the wire.
Allow to dry.

3. Attach a tiny ball of paste onto the rounded end of the column to represent the anther cap. Divide the ball into two sections.

Labellum (Throat Petal or Lip)

4. Roll out some white flower paste, leaving a thick ridge down the centre (this will give the throat some support). Cut out the petal using the throat petal cutter. Place into the wide amaryllis veiner and press firmly. Remove the petal from the mould and place back onto the board.

5. Frill the edge of the petal using the silk veining tool (you may find it easier to place the petal over your index finger to do this). Place the petal onto a pad and hollow out the throat using a metal ball tool. Moisten the bottom edges of the petal. Position the column with the hollowed side down against the petal and carefully pull the sides of the petal up against the column. Do not overlap the two edges over the column or obstruct the wire. Curl the edges of the petal back.

6. Make sure that there is some space between the column and the centre of the petal by pushing a paintbrush handle (or similar) into it. Neaten the petal around the base of the column and remove any excess paste.

Lateral Petals (Wing Petals)

7. Roll out some more white paste, leaving a thick ridge for the wire. Cut out a wing petal shape. Insert a moistened 26-gauge wire into about a third to half the length of the petal. Soften the edges and then vein using the Stargazer B petal veiner.

8. Pinch the petal from the front to the back to create a ridged effect on the front of the petal. Bend and form the petal so that it will curve forwards in the flower. Repeat to make an opposite lateral petal. Allow to firm up a little before the next stage.

9. Tape the two lateral petals into either side of the throat and column using half-width white floristry tape. If the paste is still pliable you will be able to reshape them to create a more realistic effect.

Sepals

10. This is the most difficult part of the flower to make as the three petals are actually fused together to form one, making it quite difficult to position them comfortably. Roll out a piece of white flower paste, not too thinly. Leave a thicker ridge at the centre to provide support. Cut out the sepal shape, positioning the central petal over the ridge in the paste.

11. Soften the edges of the three sepals and vein each one using the Stargazer B veiner. Moisten the centre of the shape and thread the wired petals/throat section through the centre. Carefully wrap the paste around the back of the flower. Pinch off any excess paste. Curl and pinch each sepal back slightly.

Take a small piece of sponge and cut a slit down the middle. Place this behind the petals to give them some support until they have firmed up enough to hold their own weight.

Colouring

12. Dust the base of each petal and sepal with a light mixture of Vine and Edelweiss Dust Food Colours. Mix together African violet and plum craft dusts and colour the petals, throat and sepals from the edges in towards each petal.

13. Paint a dark patch of colour using Cyclamen Liquid Food Colour mixed with some aubergine craft dust. Use a fine paintbrush to apply and control the colour in the throat.

Buds

14. These are a very odd shape to make in sugar. Roll a ball of white flower paste into a teardrop shape. Pinch the tip into a sharp point and curve slightly. Stroke the sides to flatten them a little, representing the three outer sepals.

15. Pinch a small spur at the base of the bud using your finger and thumb. Insert a hooked, moistened 26-gauge wire into the base of the bud just behind the spur. Divide the surface of the bud into three using a plain-edge cutting wheel. Dust to a much paler version of the flower. Repeat to make several buds.

Tape over each stem with half-width white floristry tape.

Leaves

16. Roll out some Holly/Ivy coloured flower paste quite thickly, leaving a thicker ridge for the wire. Cut out a freehand leaf shape using the plain-edge cutting wheel. Insert a moistened 26 or 24-gauge wire into the ridge. Soften the edge with a ball tool.

17. Draw a central vein down the leaf using the cutting wheel. Pinch the back of the leaf heavily to create a ridge and also to emphasize the central vein on the front of the leaf. Curve the leaf slightly whilst the paste is still soft.

18. Dust with Forest Green, Holly/Ivy, Leaf Green and Vine Dust Food Colours. Dip into half-strength confectioners' glaze. Tape with half-width Nile green floristry tape.

Carnation

The botanical name for carnations is *Dianthus*, which translated from Greek means "divine"! Carnations were one of the very first flowers I was ever taught to make in sugar. They are easy and effective flowers for the beginner to make. However, you must be careful to combine them with other lighter flowers to balance out the dense head of carnation petals. The carnation is currently in fashion and there is a huge array of colours and patterned flower heads available. I prefer to make the flower with individual petals rather than with the more familiar round, scalloped carnation cutter.

Materials

Pale Holly/Ivy coloured and white flower paste

22, 30 and 33-gauge white wires

Nile green floristry tape

SK Edelweiss, Forest Green, Holly/Ivy, Leaf Green and Vine Dust Food Colours

Equipment

Nasturtium petal cutter: 447 (TT) *or* carnation cutter: 346 (TT) *or* carnation petal templates (see page 140)

Fine-nosed pliers

Dresden tool (Jem)

Ceramic silk veining tool (HP)

Large stephanotis cutter: 556 (TT) *or* small nasturtium calyx cutter: 661 (TT)

CelStick (CC) (optional)

Flower Centre

1. Bend a hook in the end of a 22-gauge wire. Attach a small amount of the coloured paste you intend to make the petals with; in this case I have added a small amount of Vine Dust Food Colour to white flower paste to make a creamy-green colour. Squash the paste onto the hook and flatten it slightly. Stamens can also be added at this stage, however, they are usually only seen in a mature flower so I leave them out. Allow to dry a little before the next stage.

Petals

2. Bend the nasturtium cutter into shape by squeezing in the pointed end to make a more elongated, elegant shape. Fine-nosed pliers are useful for this. Alternatively, use the templates on page 140. You might prefer to use a larger, single petal carnation cutter to make the larger flowers.

3. Roll out some pale creamy-green flower paste and cut out several petals. I don't count the petals or layers, I just keep adding petals until I have created the size of flower required. Work the rounded edge of each petal, using the broad end of a Dresden tool to 'double frill' the edge and also create a veined effect on the petals. Add extra veining and softer frilling with the silk veining tool.

4. Cut into the edge of the petal using either the fine end of the Dresden tool or a sharp scalpel to create the characteristic fringed edges. Hold each petal in turn and crease them slightly before you attach them to the centre.

5. Make a sugar glue from egg white (see Important Note on page 133) and flower paste blended together on the edge of the board. Use the broad end of the Dresden tool to stick the petals onto the dried centre. Start to attach the petals tightly at first around the dried centre, adding extra creases as you work to give the flower some character. Continue to add petals until you have created the size of flower you require. Try not to spiral the petals down the flower as this will create a pointed effect; aim for a flatter flower head. Flick the edges of the petals to add more interest and open up the outer petals to allow them to 'breathe'. Allow to dry before adding the calyx.

Calyx

6. Knead a ball of pale green flower paste to make it smooth and pliable. Mould the ball into a teardrop shape and pinch out the base to form the shape of a golf tee. Place the shape flat against the board and roll out the paste to thin it slightly. To cut out the calyx shape, place the golf tee on top of the stephanotis cutter and roll over the paste onto the edge of the cutter with a CelStick or ceramic tool. This method avoids the problem of getting the calyx stuck in the cutter.

7. Open up the centre of the calyx using the pointed end of the ceramic tool. Next, press the sides of the calyx against the tool to thin them out and hollow out the calyx shape. Soften and broaden each of the five sepals by rolling them out against the board, leaving the centre of each sepal slightly thicker.

8. Draw a central vein down each sepal using the Dresden tool. Hollow them out a little using a small ball tool.

9. Moisten the back of the flower and thread the calyx onto it. Round off and trim away the excess paste from the calyx using a pair of sharp scissors. Turn the flower upside-down and cut two sets of two sepals into the base of the calyx using a fine pair of sharp scissors.

Thicken the stem with half-width Nile green floristry tape.

Colouring

10. Colour the petals with a light mixture of Vine and Edelweiss Dust Food Colours. Dust the calyx with a mixture of Edelweiss, Forest Green, Holly/Ivy and Leaf Green Dust Food Colours.

Leaves

These are not essential if you are planning to wire the flowers into a spray or bouquet. If you intend to display them in an arrangement or vase then you will need to add them.

11. Blend a sausage of pale green flower paste onto a 33 or 30-gauge wire, depending on the size of leaf you are making. Thin the base and the tip into a point. Place the shape against the board and flatten it using the flat side of a silicone veiner (or similar). If the shape does not resemble a carnation leaf, trim it to shape with a pair of scissors and soften the edge slightly. Pinch the leaf to create a central vein and curve a little. Dust in the same way as for the calyx.

Tape the leaves onto the stem in pairs.

Clary Sage

Materials

22, 26, 28 and 30-gauge white wires

Holly/Ivy coloured and white flower paste

SK Edelweiss, Forest Green, Holly/Ivy and Vine Dust Food Colours

SK Glaze Cleaner (Isopropyl Alcohol)

African violet and plum craft dusts

Nile green floristry tape

Equipment

Plain-edge cutting wheel (PME)

Dendrobium Montrose orchid lip petal cutter: 848 (TT)

Small ornamental nettle veiner or SK Great Impressions Hydrangea Petal Veiner (large)

Dresden tool (Jem)

Sage leaf veiner (CCUT)

Fine paintbrush

The decorative pink, purple or green-tinged modified bracts of this plant tend to shadow both the flowers and the green foliage of clary sage (*Salvia viridis*). The instructions given here describe only the bracts and leaves of the plant, making it simpler to use in bouquets and arrangements.

Bract Buds

1. Bend a hook in the end of a 26-gauge white wire. Mould a ball of white flower paste into a cone shape and insert the moistened hook into the broad end. Thin down the base onto the wire to make it slightly pointed at both ends. Divide into two leaf-bract sections using either a sharp scalpel or a plain-edge cutting wheel. Pinch a ridge down the middle of both bracts to represent the ridged veining on the back of the leaf.

Bracts

2. Roll out some white flower paste, leaving a thick ridge down the centre for the wire. Cut out a bract shape using the Dendrobium Montrose orchid lip cutter.

Insert a moistened 30 or 28-gauge wire into the thick ridge.

3. Soften the edge of the bract. Place in a hydrangea petal (bract) or ornamental nettle veiner to texture the paste. Pinch the bract down the centre to emphasize the central vein. Allow to firm up a little before colouring. Repeat to make the bracts in pairs. To vary the size of the bracts you may either cut out the shape using the lip cutter, and then re-align the cutter to re-cut and reduce the shape in size, or simply cut out a bract shape freehand using a sharp scalpel or plain-edge cutting wheel.

Leaves

4. Roll out some green flower paste to make the actual leaves of the plant. Cut the leaves out freehand using a plain-edge cutting wheel. Insert a 28-gauge wire into the thick ridge. Create a jagged edge using the broad end of the Dresden tool to pull out the paste against the board. Vein using a fresh sage leaf or commercial veiner.

Colouring

5. Mix some Holly/Ivy with a touch of Forest Green Dust Food Colour. Dilute with isopropyl alcohol and paint some fine lines on the back and front of each bract; you do not need to follow the exact veining left by the veiner. Dust the edges of each bract with your chosen colour (Vine, plum or African violet mixed with some Edelweiss). Dust the foliage with a mixture of Edelweiss, Forest Green, Holly/Ivy and tinges of the bract colour on the edge.

6. Tape the bracts in pairs, starting tight against the leaf bract. Add a 22-gauge wire to elongate and strengthen the stem and tape in place with Nile green floristry tape. Continue to add the bracts in pairs, gradually adding the green foliage in pairs too.

Lotus pods can be used effectively at their fresh green stage or dried to a dark brown for dried arrangements. They are actually the seed receptacle from the centre of the fragrant pink East Indian Lotus flower (*Nelumbo nuciflora*).

Materials

Various sizes of styrofoam balls (CC)

18 and 20-gauge wires

High-tack, non-toxic craft glue

Pale Holly/Ivy coloured flower paste

Nile green floristry tape

SK Edelweiss, Forest Green, Holly/Ivy, Leaf Green and Vine Dust Food Colours

Aubergine craft dust

Quarter or half-strength SK Confectioners' Glaze

Equipment

Angled tweezers (optional)

Plain-edge cutting wheel (PME)

Ceramic silk veining tool (HP)

Scriber (PME)

Green Lotus Pods

Preparation

The lotus pod can be made in various ways. I prefer to use a styrofoam ball to build up the bulk of the pod. A hollowed out cup can also be modelled with a lid attached to form the flat surface; this is best for a dried seed pod where a seedless appearance is needed. The seeds actually drop down into the receptacle, so you might like to add some small dried balls of paste to rattle around in the pod when the whole thing is dry. However, if you are aiming to make a fresher green pod then it is easier to use a styrofoam ball to bulk up the pod.

1. Cut away about a third of a styrofoam ball to leave a flat surface. Bend a hook in the end of either a 20 or 18-gauge wire, depending on the size of pod you are intending to make. I use a mixture of sizes in arrangements and sprays. Apply some high-tack glue onto the open hook and pull it through from the flat side of the styrofoam ball to embed the hook into it. Allow to dry overnight if you have time. A low-melt glue gun may also be used to attach the two together, giving a more instant join.

Surface Application and Texture

2. Roll out some pale green flower paste so that it is quite fleshy. Apply some fresh egg white (see Important Note on page 133) onto the surface of the styrofoam and cover the whole shape with the green paste. Flatten off the top and smooth down the sides of the pod. Trim away the excess paste from the base.

3. Pinch around the top edge of the pod using your finger and thumb to form a ridge. You might need angled tweezers to add a little more definition. Continue to work down the sides of the pod making a combination of pinched ridges with the angled tweezers and extra lines with a plain-edge cutting wheel.

4. Create several holes of various sizes using both the pointed end and the rounded end of a ceramic modelling tool. Add modelled balls to the holes to represent the developing seeds. Indent the centre of each seed when they are in place using a sharp scriber. Tape over the stem several times to make it look more fleshy. Allow to dry a little before colouring.

5. Dust in layers with Forest Green, Leaf Green, Holly/Ivy, Vine and Edelweiss Dust Food Colours. A light dusting of aubergine craft dust on the pinched ridges around the top of the pod and on the sides will add a little more interest. Steam the pod, or glaze with either quarter or half-strength confectioners' glaze.

Orchid and Lotus Spray

Flowers and Foliage

9 stems of clary sage

5 Dendrobium Nobile orchids

9 carnations, various stages

3 green lotus pods

5 small vine leaves

Equipment

Pale green sisal

Crimped purple wire

Purple paper-covered wire

20-gauge wire

Wire cutters

Nile green floristry tape

Silver candleholder

Fine-nosed pliers

Preparation

1. Tease out some lengths of green sisal. Wrap the purple crimped wire around the trails to control the fibre and help form twisted and curled shapes. Curl some lengths of paper-covered wire in preparation for adding to the spray at the end. Strengthen any of the longer or heavier flowers by taping them onto 20-gauge wires with Nile green floristry tape.

Assembly

2. Form the length of the bouquet with two lengths of clary sage, one much longer than the other. The longest stem should create two thirds of the length of the spray with the shorter stem providing the remaining third. Bend the stems to a 90° angle and tape together using half-width Nile green tape. Continue to add the remaining shorter lengths of clary sage to create the rest of the outline of the spray.

3. Tape in the Dendrobium orchids using one of them as the focal point (and the highest flower) of the spray. The others should be staggered throughout the spray. Carefully adjust the position of the orchids using fine-nosed pliers.

4. Fill in the large gaps in the spray with the carnations, using the largest ones at the centre of the spray and the smallest, almost bud-like flowers at the edges. As you add the carnations, alternate them with the lotus pods. Add the small vine leaves to fill any gaps.

5. Finally, add the curled trails of twisted sisal and purple paper-covered wire. Trim off the excess stems using wire cutters. Tie the spray onto the candleholder with paper-covered wire.

I have not used carnations on a cake since about 1990, but combined with more unusual flowers they are great for filling in large spaces. Lotus pods demand plenty of room too!

Bright Yellow

Daffodils are an instant inspiration for a springtime wedding. I have used them together with twigs of yellow forsythia, pink Daphne, variegated Hebe and ivy to form a large bouquet on this cheerful, two-tiered wedding cake.

Cake and Decoration

15cm (6") and 25.5cm (10") round rich fruitcakes

Apricot glaze

1.4kg (3lb) white almond paste

Clear alcohol (e.g. white rum, cherry or orange liqueur)

1.9kg (4lb) white sugarpaste

Fine yellow ribbon to trim the cakes

Broad yellow ribbon to trim the boards

Non-toxic glue stick

Equipment

15cm (6") thin cake board

38cm (15") round cake drum

Large food-grade posy pick (HW)

Flowers and Foliage

Daffodil bouquet (see pages 30-31)

Preparation

1. Position the small cake on top of a thin cake board of the same size. Brush both cakes with apricot glaze and cover with a white almond paste. Leave to dry overnight. Moisten the surface of the almond paste with clear alcohol and cover with white sugarpaste. Use a pair of sugarpaste smoothers to achieve a smooth finish.

2. Moisten the cake drum with cooled, boiled water or clear alcohol and cover with white sugarpaste. Trim off the excess paste and smooth over the surface with a round-edged sugarpaste smoother. Transfer the large cake onto the coated board so that it sits centrally. Blend the sugarpaste at the base of the cake down to meet the paste on the board to create a neat join. Place the smaller cake on top of the base tier, and again blend the two together to form a neat join.

3. Attach a fine band of yellow ribbon around the base of both cakes using either a small amount of royal icing or a softened mixture of sugarpaste and clear alcohol. Glue a broad band of yellow ribbon to the board edge using a non-toxic glue stick.

Assembly

4. Wire up the bouquet, as described on pages 30 to 31. Insert a large food-grade posy pick into the top tier, and then position the handle of the bouquet in it.

Daffodil

Daffodils (*Narcissus*), despite being seasonal, are one of the world's best selling cut flowers. There are many cultivated varieties available today, although it was the Romans who first brought the original wild sorts into cultivation.

Materials

20, 22, 26, 28 and 33-gauge white wires

Pale Daffodil and Holly/Ivy coloured flower paste

SK Daffodil, Forest Green, Holly/Ivy, Leaf Green, Sunflower and Vine Dust Food Colours

Nile green and white floristry tape

Cream craft dust

Half-strength SK Confectioners' Glaze

Equipment

Wire cutters

Plain-edged, angled tweezers

Plain-edge cutting wheel (PME)

Daffodil cutters (or templates, see page 140)

Sharp scalpel

Ceramic silk veining tool (HP)

Dresden tool (Jem)

Medium CelStick (CC)

SK Great Impressions Stargazer B Veiner

Sharp scissors

SK Great Impressions Tulip leaf veiner

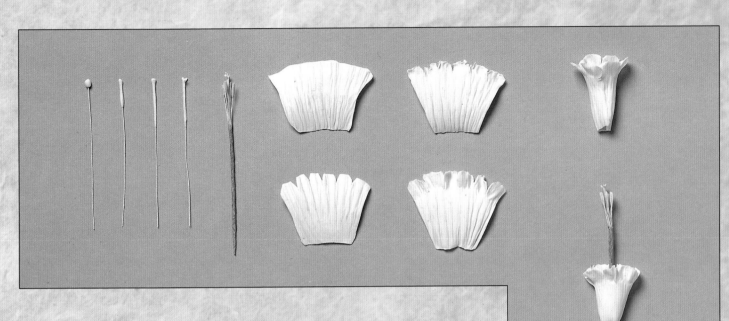

Pistil

1. Cut a short length of 28-gauge white wire. Blend a little Daffodil coloured flower paste onto the end. Try to form a 'bead' at the top and then thin the paste down onto the wire. Flatten the tip. Pinch into three sections using plain-edged, angled tweezers. Allow to dry. Dust the tip lightly with Vine Dust Food Colour.

Stamens

2. Cut six short lengths of 33-gauge white wire. Blend a tiny piece of yellow paste onto the end of each to represent the anthers. Draw a line down either side using the plain-edge cutting wheel.

Tape the six stamens around the pistil and onto a 22-gauge wire. The pistil should stand a little higher than the stamens. Dust the anthers with a mixture of Sunflower and Daffodil Dust Food Colours. Dust the filaments with Vine.

Corolla (Trumpet)

3. Roll out some pale Daffodil coloured flower paste so that it is quite fleshy. Cut out the corolla shape using either a cutter or a template and sharp scalpel. Create the ridged veining by simply pressing the silk veining tool onto the petal in a fan formation. Try not to work the paste too much as this will make it much bigger than its original size. Turn it over and add some more ridged veining. If the petal does become huge then you will need to re-cut it back into shape with the cutter or scalpel.

4. Using a sharp scalpel, cut into the edge to form six sections. Remove narrow 'V' shapes of paste. Work each section using the broad end of a Dresden tool to double frill the edge. Re-frill the edge using the silk veining tool.

5. Moisten one edge of the shape and join the two side edges together to form a trumpet. Push a medium sized CelStick through the trumpet to blend the join in the petal. Press firmly with your thumb against the paste. Add extra ridged veining if you have wiped them out in the joining process.

6. Gather the base of the trumpet and join it together. Use the rounded end of the CelStick to help form the shape. Moisten the base of the stamens and thread them through the trumpet. Pinch around the base of the petal to secure it to the wire. Curl the edges back slightly. Allow to dry a little before colouring.

Petals and Sepals

7. There are three petals and three sepals that form the outer layer of a daffodil. There is often a slight difference in size between the two, however, the flower I chose to copy had sepals and petals roughly the same size as each other. Roll out some pale Daffodil coloured flower paste, leaving a thick ridge down the centre for the wire. Cut out the sepal/petal shape using the outer cutter or the template. Insert a moistened 28-gauge white wire into the ridge. Soften the edge of the petal/sepal using a medium metal ball tool. Vein using the Stargazer B petal veiner. Add extra veins using the fine end of the Dresden tool if desired. Pinch the petal from the base to the tip. Repeat to make the three inner petals and three outer sepals. Allow to dry a little before assembling the flower.

Assembly

8. Tape the three inner petals tightly around the base of the corolla using half-width Nile green floristry tape. Add and tape the three outer sepals slightly behind and in-between the petals. If the paste is still slightly soft you should be able to manipulate the petals to create a more realistic finish.

9. Form a cone of paste and thread this onto the back of the flower. Squeeze the paste up against the petals/sepals and thin down the back slightly. Blend the paste onto the back of the petals using the broad end of the Dresden tool. A little cooled, boiled water or clear alcohol will help to dissolve the sugar slightly and disguise the join in the petals, but be careful not to make the paste too wet. Allow to dry.

10. Add a small ball of paste to the back of the flower at the base to represent the ovary. Pinch it against the flower to make them look like they belong to each other.

Colouring

11. Dust the flower using a mixture of Daffodil, Sunflower and Edelweiss Dust Food Colours. I tend to make the corolla slightly stronger in colour. Catch the edges of the petals and sepals to give them a lighter appearance. Dust the ovary and up onto the back of the flower with a mixture of Leaf Green and Vine Dust Food Colours. Add some Vine to the base of the corolla just below the stamens – this helps to draw your eye to the centre of the flower. Tinge the tips of the sepals and petals lightly with Vine if desired.

12. Tape the flower onto a 20-gauge wire and tape over several times with half or even full-width tape. Polish the tape using the side of a pair of scissors to help blend the overlapping tape. Bend the flower head over slightly.

13. Add a papery spathe around the ovary at the base of the flower. I prefer to use white floristry tape dusted with cream craft dust for this. Cut a pointed bract shape using sharp scissors and dust with cream craft dust. Using the fine end of the Dresden tool, create a series of veins on the tape. Stretch the tape as you work to enhance the papery appearance. Wrap around the base of the ovary and tape over the base of the spathe with a little more green tape. Daffodil stems are actually flattened slightly, so carefully roll over the stem with a rolling pin.

14. Dust the stem with Forest Green and Holly/Ivy Dust Food Colours. Seal the colour and tape with some non-toxic craft glue. This will dry clear and give a slight, realistic-looking shine to the stem.

Buds

15. Bend a hook in the end of a 22 or 20-gauge wire. Form a long cone shape of pale yellow flower paste and insert the moistened, hooked wire into the base. Thin down the back of the bud to elongate it and trim away any excess paste. Divide the bud into three sections using the plain-edge cutting wheel. Add an ovary and colour in the same way as for the flower. Over-dust with Vine and Leaf Green Dust Food Colours. Add a spathe, as for the flower.

Leaves

16. Roll out some Holly/Ivy coloured flower paste, leaving a long, thick ridge down the centre. Cut out a long, slender, strap-shaped leaf using the plain-edge cutting wheel. Insert a 26, 24 or 22-gauge wire into the leaf, depending upon the leaf size. Soften the edge slightly. Vein using a tulip leaf veiner or a packet of 33-gauge wires which have been curved to follow the line of the leaf. Pinch and re-shape the leaf. Allow to firm up a little before dusting.

17. Dust in layers with Forest Green, Holly/Ivy, Leaf Green and Vine Dust Food Colours. Dip into half-strength confectioners' glaze.

Forsythia

Forsythia, sometimes known as the 'Golden Bell', is a flowering shrub originally from China. The plant has become one of the most popular shrubs for British gardens. The flowering, twiggy stems can also be bought as a cut flower from November to March. The flowers, which may be cream through to golden yellow, appear on the branches before the foliage begins to fully develop.

Materials

22, 28, 30 and 33-gauge white wires

Pale Daffodil coloured flower paste

SK Daffodil, Edelweiss, Leaf Green, Sunflower and Vine Dust Food Colours

Brown and Nile green floristry tape

Equipment

Wire cutters

Sharp scissors

Fine-nosed pliers

Fuchsia sepal cutter: 340 (TT)

CelStick (CC)

Dresden tool (Jem)

Plain-edge cutting wheel (PME)

Pistil

1. Cut a short length of 28-gauge white wire. Blend a tiny piece of pale Daffodil flower paste onto the end of the wire. Form a point at the tip of the pistil. Work the base into a point, too. Split the pistil in half lengthways using a sharp pair of scissors. Squeeze the two sections back together. Allow to dry.

Flower

2. Using a pair of fine-nosed pliers, squeeze each sepal of the cutter together to form narrower shapes for the forsythia flower. (I also find that this finer shape makes a better fuchsia!) Mould a ball of pale yellow paste into a cone shape. Pinch out the base to form a hat shape. The back of the flower should be quite short. Roll out the brim of the 'hat' using a CelStick.

3. Cut out the flower shape using the narrowed fuchsia sepal cutter. Remove the flower from the cutter and open up the throat using the pointed end of a CelStick. Place the flower upside-down on the board and elongate each of the sepals by rolling over the paste with the CelStick. Try not to roll the petals too finely as this will make it difficult to form a good shape.

4. Place the flower upside-down on a pad and hollow out the back of each petal using the broad end of a Dresden tool. Use a stroking action to hollow the whole length of each petal. Pinch each petal back slightly at the tip. Moisten the base of the dried pistil and pull the wire through the centre of the flower. The back of the flower should be quite short, so trim away any excess length if necessary. Snip into the base of the flower a few times to create a representation of the calyx.

Buds

5. Cut short lengths of 33 and 30-gauge wires, depending upon the size of bud you are making. Roll a ball of pale yellow flower paste and then form into a teardrop shape. Insert a moistened wire into the base of the teardrop and thin down the base of the bud onto the wire. Divide into four sections using a pair of sharp scissors or the plain-edge cutting wheel. Snip a calyx in the same way as for the flower.

Repeat to make numerous buds in varying sizes.

Colouring and Assembly

6. Dust the flowers and buds to the required depth of yellow using a mixture of Sunflower and Daffodil Dust Food Colours with a touch of Edelweiss. Dust the calyces with a mixture of Vine and Leaf Green Dust Food Colours. Add a touch of green to the pistil.

Tape the buds and flowers in groups onto a 22 or 20-gauge wire using brown tape. Add some new growth foliage using small strips of green floristry tape cut to shape. Simply tape leaves onto the stem from the same point as the flowers and buds.

Daphne

There are around fifty species of Daphne from Europe and cooler parts of Asia. The shrub produces highly scented clusters of flowers that can be white, cream, green, pink, purple tinged or red.

Materials

Fine, white stamens

22, 26, 28, 30 and 33-gauge white wires

High-tack, non-toxic craft glue

SK Daffodil, Forest Green, Holly/Ivy, Leaf Green and Sunflower Dust Food Colours

Mid-Holly/Ivy coloured and white flower paste

CelStick (CC)

African violet, aubergine and plum craft dusts

Nile green floristry tape

Half-strength SK Confectioners' Glaze

Equipment

Daphne cutters: 285, 466 (TT)

Smooth ceramic tool (HP)

Dresden tool (Jem)

Sharp, curved scissors

Plain-edge cutting wheel (PME)

SK Great Impressions Bittersweet Leaf Veiner

Sharp scalpel

Stamens

1. Cut four short stamen lengths. Attach to the end of a 30-gauge wire using a tiny amount of high-tack, non-toxic craft glue and allow to dry. Trim off the tips. Moisten the cut ends with fresh egg white (see Important Note on page 133) or edible glue and dip into a mixture of Sunflower and Daffodil Dust Food Colours. Allow to dry.

Flower

2. Form a ball of well-kneaded white flower paste into a teardrop. Pinch around the broad end of the shape with your fingers and thumbs to create a brim. Roll out the brim using a CelStick. Cut out the flower using your chosen size of Daphne cutter. I have used the larger of the two sizes for the flowers pictured here.

3. Open up the centre of the flower using the pointed end of a smooth ceramic tool. Place the flower against your index finger and, using the ceramic tool, broaden each of the petals.

4. Apply a little pressure onto the edges of the petals with a Dresden tool to curl them in slightly. Pinch the tips of each petal and then thread the wired stamens through the centre of the flower. Thin down the back and trim if necessary.

Buds

5. I tend to use far more buds than flowers in each group as they are simpler and quicker to make. Form a small teardrop of white flower paste and insert a 33 or 30-gauge wire (depending upon the size of the bud you are making) into the broad end. Thin down the neck of the bud onto the wire. Hold the top half of the bud between two fingers and a thumb to create a three-sided bud. Next, divide the bud in half using a sharp pair of scissors. Curve the shape slightly.

6. Dust the backs of the flowers and each bud heavily with a mixture of plum, a touch of African violet and aubergine craft dusts. Dust the base of each bud and flower with Leaf Green Dust Food Colours. Tape them into tight clusters.

Leaves

7. Roll out some mid-green flower paste, leaving a thick ridge down the centre. Cut out a freehand leaf shape using the plain-edge cutting wheel. Insert a moistened 28 or 26-gauge wire into the thick ridge. Soften the edge and vein using a bittersweet leaf veiner. Pinch the leaf from the wire to the tip to accentuate the central vein.

8. Dust the edge lightly with aubergine. Over-dust in layers of Forest Green, Holly/Ivy and Leaf Green Dust Food Colours. Allow to dry, then dip into half-strength confectioners' glaze. The central veining is often much paler than the main part of the leaf; to achieve this effect, simply etch away the veins using a sharp scalpel blade.

Tape the leaves in a spiral around each flower cluster using Nile green floristry tape. Dust the stems with a mixture of aubergine and Holly/Ivy dusts.

Hebe

There are many species and hybrid forms of ornamental Hebe from New Zealand, Australia, New Guinea and South America. I have chosen to use only the foliage of the plant as the flowers are tiny and tedious to make!

New Growth

1. Colour some flower paste with a touch of Vine and Daffodil Dust Food Colours. Roll a ball of well-kneaded paste and then mould it into a teardrop shape. Insert a hooked, moistened 24-gauge wire into the broad base of the teardrop. Work the paste down onto the wire. Snip the shape in half using a pair of sharp scissors. Squeeze the two sections back together to represent two leaves beginning to form. Pinch a slight ridge down the centre of each.

Leaves

2. The leaves grow opposite each other in pairs, graduating in size very slightly down the stem. Roll out some more of the pale creamy-green flower paste, leaving a thick ridge for the wire. The leaves can be quite fleshy so bear this in mind when you roll the paste out. Cut out the leaf shape freehand using a sharp scalpel or plain-edge cutting wheel. Insert a moistened 30 or 28-gauge white wire into the ridge.

3. Soften the edge of the leaf slightly using a medium metal ball tool. Hollow out the back of the leaf. Draw down a central vein using the plain-edge cutting wheel. Repeat to make lots of leaves, pairing them by size as you work.

Colouring and Assembly

4. Tinge the edges of the leaves and new growth with a mixture of plum and aubergine craft dusts mixed together. Paint the variegated colouring onto each of the leaves in layers. Mix together some Vine, Leaf Green and Holly/Ivy Dust Food Colours with a touch of isopropyl alcohol. Add a little Edelweiss Dust Food Colour. Start by painting in some paler markings. Gradually increase the Holly/Ivy and add a touch of Forest Green to make a darker colouring. Dip into half-strength confectioners' glaze or spray with an edible spray varnish.

5. Tape two leaves behind the new growth, then continue to tape down the stem with half-width Nile green tape. Continue to add the leaves in pairs down the stem. Dust the stem with the aubergine/plum mixture used on the leaves.

Materials

Pale cream coloured flower paste

SK Daffodil, Edelweiss, Forest Green, Holly/Ivy, Leaf Green and Vine Dust Food Colours

24, 28 and 30-gauge wires

Aubergine and plum craft dusts

SK Glaze Cleaner (Isopropyl Alcohol)

Half-strength SK Confectioners' Glaze or edible spray varnish

Nile green floristry tape

Equipment

Sharp scissors

Plain-edge cutting wheel (PME)

Medium ball tool (CC)

Daffodil Bouquet

Flowers and Foliage

5 stems of forsythia

7 stems of ivy (see pages 74-75)

7 daffodils

3 stems of Daphne

3 stems of Hebe foliage

Equipment

18 and 20-gauge wires

Wire cutters

Nile green floristry tape

Fine-nosed pliers

Stems of forsythia form the main structure of this bouquet, while ivy softens the edges of the display.

Preparation

1. Strengthen any flower or foliage stems that need it by taping a 20 or 18-gauge wire alongside the main stem using half-width Nile green floristry tape.

Assembly

2. Bend the two longest stems of forsythia to a 90° angle and tape them together. This will form both the length and a handle for the bouquet. Tape in the other shorter stems of forsythia to create the width and more of the intended shape of the bouquet.

Soften the edges of the bouquet by adding lengths of trailing ivy leaves. Curve the stems as you work to create more movement.

3. Next, tape in the biggest and best daffodil to form the focal point of the bouquet. This flower should stand proud of all the others. Continue to add the remaining daffodils to fill in the main area of the spray.

4. Use the variegated pink-tinged Hebe foliage and clusters of Daphne flowers to fill in the remaining gaps of the bouquet. Trim away excess wires as you work. Use fine-nosed pliers to help thread the smaller flowers behind the daffodils.

Tape over the handle of the bouquet with full-width Nile green tape to neaten it.

Young Hearts

Pomegranates are used as fertility symbols in some cultures, making them a perfect wedding cake decoration.

Cake and Decoration

25.5cm (10") heart shaped rich fruitcake

Apricot glaze

1.25kg (2¾lb) white almond paste

Clear alcohol (e.g. white rum, cherry or orange liqueur)

1.4kg (3lb) sugarpaste

SK Poppy Paste Food Colour

15cm (6") heart shaped dummy cake

Fine orange ribbon to trim the cakes

Broad nude ribbon to trim the board

Non-toxic glue stick

Brown floristry tape

Equipment

35.5cm (14") heart shaped cake drum

2 food-grade posy picks (W)

2 food-grade plastic dowels (optional)

Flowers and Foliage

3 pomegranate flowers

12 pomegranate buds

3 pomegranate fruits

45 pomegranate leaves

Preparation

1. I have used a polystyrene dummy cake for the top tier of this design as it is lighter and easier to balance than a real cake. You can, however, use a real cake if preferred. Brush the larger heart shaped fruitcake with apricot glaze and cover with white almond paste. Leave to dry at least overnight. Brush the surface of the almond paste with clear alcohol and cover with very pale SK Poppy coloured sugarpaste. Smooth over the surface using a pair of sugarpaste smoothers to achieve a neat finish. Moisten the base drum with a very thin coating of clear alcohol and cover with sugarpaste. Place the cake on top of the board and blend the two together around the base of the cake using a smoother. A pad of sugarpaste pressed into the palm of your hand can be useful for smoothing the top edges and difficult areas of the shape.

2. Brush the heart shaped polystyrene dummy cake with clear alcohol, cover with sugarpaste and leave to dry for several days. Moisten the base of the dummy with alcohol. Roll out some more sugarpaste and place the dummy cake on top. Using a sharp knife, trim away the excess paste from the edge. Carefully turn the cake up onto one side and position it on top of the coated fruitcake. I used a small amount of sugarpaste softened with clear alcohol to hold the cake in position – you might prefer to use a couple of sharpened food grade plastic dowels to hold the two tiers together (particularly if you have used two fruitcakes).

3. Attach a thin band of orange ribbon around the base of each cake, using a tiny amount of softened sugarpaste to hold it in place. Attach a broader band of nude coloured ribbon to the board edge using a non-toxic glue stick.

Flower Sprays

4. Wire up three sprays of pomegranate buds, flowers, fruit and foliage (see pages 38 to 39) using brown floristry tape. Insert a posy pick into the top of the larger cake to hold the spray. The spray on the top tier is simply pushed directly into the coated polystyrene dummy cake. However, if you are using a real cake for the top tier then you will need to insert the flowers into a pick as for the base tier. The flowers at the base of the wedding cake are simply placed on the table close to the cake.

The pomegranate (*Punica*), which can be a tree or shrub, has been valued since ancient times; in fact, its seeds have been found in Bronze Age Jericho. The fruit has long been used as a fertility symbol as the seeds actually contain oestrone. There are two species of pomegranate, one can be found from the eastern Mediterranean area to the Himalayas, the other is restricted to the island of Socotra.

Materials

White seed head stamens

High-tack, non-toxic craft glue

18, 20, 26, 28 and 30-gauge white wires

SK Daffodil, Forest Green, Holly/Ivy, Sunflower and Vine Dust Food Colours

Aubergine, coral and ruby craft dusts

Pale Daffodil coloured, mid Holly/Ivy coloured and white flower paste

Brown and Nile green floristry tape

Half-strength SK Confectioners' Glaze or edible spray varnish

3cm and 4cm (1$^1/_2$" and 1$^1/_4$") styrofoam balls (CC)

Sisal (available from florists)

Equipment

Rose petal cutters: 278, 279 (TT)

Ceramic silk veining tool (HP)

CelStick (CC)

Six petal pointed blossom cutters: N3, N4 (OP)

Ball tool (CC)

Plain-edge cutting wheel (PME)

SK Great Impressions Briar Rose Leaf Veiner (large)

Pomegranate

Flower Stamens

1. Glue together about six to eight seed head stamens to form a small group using non-toxic craft glue. Work the glue from the centre of each group to towards the tips, leaving enough length unglued on either end of the stamens to create some movement. Allow the groups to dry a little but not set completely. Cut them in half and trim off the excess to leave shorter individual groups. Apply a little glue to the end of a 26-gauge wire and carefully attach the first group. Squeeze the stamens onto the wire to secure them (the glue sets quite quickly). Continue to add other groups until you have created the desired look (usually about five or six groups altogether).

2. Dust the tips (anthers) of the stamens with a mixture of Daffodil and Sunflower Dust Food Colours. Dust the length of the stamens (filaments) with coral craft dust.

Petals

3. The number of petals can vary between species and cultivated varieties. Roll out some white flower paste thinly, leaving a fine ridge for the wire (a grooved board may also be used). Cut out the petal shape using a rose petal cutter (either of the two listed opposite, depending on the size of flower you intend to make). Insert a moistened 30-gauge white wire into the thick ridge of the petal at the pointed end.

4. Place the petal back onto the board and vein the petal in a fan formation using the silk veining tool. Aim the point of the tool at the point of the petal and use short rolling actions so that you vein and widen the petal slightly. Increase the pressure at the rounded edge of the petal to frill it. Pinch the petal at the base and then set it to one side to firm up before colouring. The petals are quite crinkly on the real flower so you might prefer to crinkle the sugar petals too. Repeat to make five to seven petals per flower.

5. The petals are usually a coral/red colour, although there is a rare version with white petals. I prefer the stronger coloured flowers so I have dusted the petals heavily with coral craft dust, fading out a little towards the edges. Add a little extra depth at the base of each petal by dusting with a mixture of ruby and coral dusts.

6. Tape five to seven petals around the stamens using half-width Nile green floristry tape. Try to keep the stamens short in the flower. If the petals are still slightly pliable it will give you a chance to decide how mature and open you want the flower to be.

Calyx

7. The calyx is thick and fleshy, just like the fruit. In fact it is this heavy back of the flower that will form the pomegranate fruit once pollinated. The number of

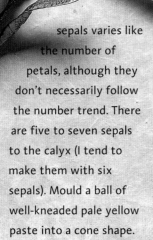

sepals varies like the number of petals, although they don't necessarily follow the number trend. There are five to seven sepals to the calyx (I tend to make them with six sepals). Mould a ball of well-kneaded pale yellow paste into a cone shape.

Pinch out the broad end of the cone to form a pointed hat shape. Place it on the board and roll out the brim of the 'hat' using a CelStick. The paste should still be quite fleshy.

8. It is impossible to get a cutter over the heavy back of the calyx to cut out the sepal shape. The easiest method is to place the brim of the 'hat' against one of the six-petal blossom cutters and roll over each sepal with a CelStick to cut through the paste. Remove the excess paste from the edges of the cutter. Soften the edges of each sepal slightly using a ball tool. Open up the centre of the calyx using the CelStick or the pointed end of a smooth ceramic tool. Press each sepal against the tool to hollow it out a little.

9. Thin down the base of the calyx and thread it onto the back of the flower. Push the sepals up against the flower, and then continue to thin down the calyx a little more. The calyx is almost divided into four sections; broaden and thin out each section and then create a slightly rounded, tapered base on the stem. Mark in-between each sepal using a plain-edge cutting wheel to continue the sepals into the main body of the calyx.

10. Dust the calyx with coral and ruby craft dusts. The colour can be very strong or fading out towards the tips of the sepals. Spray the calyx with an edible glaze or dip into half or three quarter-strength confectioners' glaze.

Buds

11. Bend a hook in the end of a 28 or 26-gauge wire. Mould a ball of paste into a cone shape. Insert the hooked wire into the broad end of the cone. Thin out the four sections described above. They are not quite as developed on the smaller buds. Divide the tip of the bud into six to represent the sepals; use a cage (see page 139), sharp scalpel or plain-edge cutting wheel to divide the bud equally. Repeat to make buds in various sizes. Tape over each stem with Nile green floristry tape.

Dust as for the calyx on the flower. Add a tinge of Vine to the very tip.

Leaves

12. The leaves are oblong to elliptical in shape and can be very bright or dark in colour. Roll out some green flower paste, leaving a thick ridge down the centre. Cut out a leaf freehand using the plain-edge cutting wheel. Insert a 28 or 26-gauge wire, depending on the size of the leaf. Soften the edge. Vein using a large Briar rose leaf veiner. Pinch down the length of the leaf to accentuate the central vein.

13. Dust with Forest Green, Holly/Ivy and Vine Dust Food Colours. Tinge the edge slightly with ruby and aubergine craft dusts mixed together. Dip into half-strength confectioners' glaze. Tape over a short length of the wire at the base of the leaf with quarter-width Nile green tape.

Fruit

The size of the fully ripened fruit varies between the two species of *Punica* and the many cultivated varieties. I have chosen a smaller fruit to make them more suited to cake decoration. The exact colour of the fruit can vary too, from yellow to reddish brown when ripe.

14. Bend a large hook in the end of a 20-gauge wire. Apply some non-toxic craft glue and pull the wire through a styrofoam ball, embedding the hook tightly into it. Allow to dry.

15. Roll out some pale yellow flower paste quite thickly. Moisten the surface of the wired ball and cover the ball with paste. Smooth out the creases and wrinkles as you work.

16. Some fruits have angled ridges to them, others do not. I tend to use the rolling pin to smooth the surface; this also leaves sides and ridges. Texture the surface in places with another styrofoam ball. Indent the top of the fruit to make way for the calyx.

17. There are two ways of making the calyx, the first of which is to cut a crown shape from pale yellow flower paste (as shown here). The second, and slightly easier method, is to use one of the six-petal pointed cutters used for the calyx on the back of the flower. Cut out the calyx shape using your preferred method and roll out the base slightly.

18. Soften the sepals and open up the centre using the rounded end of a ceramic tool. Moisten the indentation on the fruit very slightly. Position the calyx on top and embed the rounded end of the ceramic tool into it to join the two together. Use a rolling action on the side of the calyx, blending the join between the two a little more.

19. Use sisal to create the left over dead stamens in the  fruit; if you cannot get hold of this, you can use thread or fine stamens. Glue the ends together and push them into the calyx. Trim off the excess and arrange them to create a 'dead' look.

20. Dust the fruit to your preferred colour. I have layered yellows, coral, ruby and aubergine with tinges of Vine. To add extra depth to the colour of the fruit, paint on a diluted mixture of ruby and aubergine craft dusts. Mix some aubergine dust with alcohol to colour the stamens and the tips of the calyx. Spray with an edible food glaze.

Tape over the stem with Nile green tape.

21. Tape the flowers, buds and leaves onto 20 and 18-gauge wires with half-width brown tape. Group the flowers and buds and add a leaf or two where they join the branch. I have made my branches a bit stronger in appearance – the real thing has quite spindly, twiggy branches. Tape the fruit and some leaves on to separate stems. Add twisted lengths of brown tape wrapped tightly around the branch where the flowers, buds and fruit join the stem to create a more ridged bark effect.

Pomegranate Candle Arrangement

Many of the people I have made cakes for like to keep the flowers as a reminder of their special day. Here is a suggestion of how the flowers and fruit could be used as an alternative decoration. This unusual twisted candle holder, which I bought during a teaching trip to Dublin, complements the colouring of the pomegranates beautifully.

Flowers and Foliage

3 pomegranate flowers

10 pomegranate buds

3 pomegranate fruits

35 pomegranate leaves

Equipment

Ivory candle

Twisted candle holder

Fine-nosed pliers

Wire cutters

Brown floristry tape

Florists' Staysoft

Box of long matches

Preparation

1. Place the candle onto the candleholder.

Assembly

2. Tape together two informal sprays using a combination of the pomegranate fruit, flowers, buds and foliage with half or full-width brown floristry tape.

3. Attach a small amount of florists' Staysoft onto the top section of the candleholder behind the candle. Insert the smaller of the two sprays into it. Carefully rearrange the leaf stems to curve in front of the candle, making sure that none of the items are too close to the wick of the candle. The larger spray is simply placed onto the base of the candle holder.

Strike a match and light the candle!

Oriental Poppy Cake

Cake and Decoration

25.5cm (10") trefoil shaped rich fruitcake

Apricot glaze

1kg (2lb) white almond paste

Clear alcohol (e.g. white rum, cherry or orange liqueur)

1.4kg (3lb) white sugarpaste

White royal icing

SK Bluegrass, Edelweiss and Fuchsia Dust Food Colours

Aqua ribbon to trim the board

Non-toxic glue stick

Nile green floristry tape

Equipment

35.5cm (14") round cake drum

Embroidery design (see page 140)

Parchment or greaseproof paper

Scriber

Piping bags

Nos. 0 and 42 piping tubes

Pliers

Wire cutters

Large food-grade posy pick (HW)

Flowers and Foliage

1 Oriental poppy

5 Oriental poppy buds

10 Oriental poppy leaves

5 stems of Nomocharis lily

5 stems of African corn lilies

A single Oriental poppy forms the focal point of the bouquet used on this single-tiered wedding cake. Aqua coloured Ixia flowers, pale pink Nomocharis lilies and a delicate piped embroidery design have been used to complement and complete this pretty cake.

Preparation

1. Brush the cake with apricot glaze and cover with almond paste. Allow to dry overnight. Moisten the surface of the almond paste with clear alcohol and cover with white sugarpaste. Use a pair of sugarpaste smoothers to create a polished finish. Cover the cake drum with sugarpaste. Transfer the cake onto it and carefully blend the two edges of sugarpaste together using a flat-edged sugarpaste smoother. Allow to dry overnight.

Side Design

2. Trace the embroidery design from page 140 onto some parchment or greaseproof paper. Place the design against the cake and scribe it into the sugarpaste surface using a scriber. Pipe the outline of the design in white royal icing using a piping bag fitted with a No. 0 piping tube. Add extra floral dots and piped leaves to complete the design. Repeat the design on the coated board and allow to dry. Dust each section lightly with Bluegrass and Fuchsia Dust Food Colours mixed with Edelweiss Dust Food Colour.

3. Pipe a shell border around the base of the cake using white royal icing in a piping bag fitted with a No. 42 shell tube. Attach a band of aqua coloured ribbon to the board edge using a non-toxic glue stick.

Floral Decoration

4. Using half-width Nile green floristry tape, attach two stems of Nomocharis lilies onto the single Oriental poppy to form the length and line through the spray. Frame the central flower with some of its foliage and buds. Fill in the remaining gaps with extra stems of lilies and the Ixia flowers. Insert the handle of the spray into a posy pick and insert it into the cake.

Oriental Poppy

Cultivated Oriental poppies (*Papaver orientale*) are now found in shades of pink, mauve, orange, red and white. They have all been bred from the four wild species from Turkey and the Causasus. I love using poppies as they create a huge impact and are relatively quick to make.

Materials

Holly/Ivy coloured and white flower paste
Small amount of green cold porcelain (optional)
18, 20, 22, 24 and 26-gauge white wires
African violet, aubergine, plum and ruby craft dusts
High-tack, non-toxic craft glue
Black or white seed head stamens
SK Blackberry, Cyclamen and Violet Liquid Food Colours
SK Edelweiss, Forest Green and Holly/Ivy Dust Food Colours
Nile green floristry tape
SK White Satin Bridal Satin Lustre Dust or SK Magic Sparkle Dust

Equipment

Angled plain-edge tweezers
Fine scissors
Fine paintbrush
Ceramic silk veining tool (HP)
Diamond Jubilee rose petal cutters: 776-778 (TT)
Metal ball tool (CC)
Kitchen paper
Scalpel or plain-edge cutting wheel (PME)
Armenian poppy leaf cutter (AP)
Poppy leaf cutter (F) (optional)
SK Great Impressions Oriental Poppy Leaf Veiner

Ovary

1. I prefer to make the ovary with cold porcelain, as this makes attaching the stamens easier. However, you can use flower paste if you prefer. Mould a ball of green paste into a cone shape and insert a hooked 22-gauge wire into the narrow end. Flatten the top.

2. Pinch a series of lines radiating from the centre using angled tweezers. Indent in-between each of the ridges using the side of a silk veining tool. Using the flat side of a brush, dust the ridges with aubergine craft dust. Glue the stamens to the ovary. (If you are using flower paste for the ovary then you will need to make a sugar glue using flower paste and fresh egg white mixed together, see Important Note on page 133.)

Stamens

3. You will need about two bunches of black stamens to complete the flower. Glue together groups of stamens, applying the glue at the centre of the stamens. Allow the stamens to set slightly. Cut the stamens in half. Apply more glue and attach the stamens around the ovary. Squeeze the stamens tightly around the ovary to form a neat ring.

4. Paint the stamens with a mixture of Blackberry, Cyclamen and Violet Liquid Food Colours just to take off the dead look of the black stamens. If you have used white stamens then you will need to use the same black mixture to colour them.

Petals

5. The Diamond Jubilee rose cutters are already quite oval in shape. However, you will need to squeeze the cutter a little more to make wider petals. Roll out some white or suitably coloured flower paste, leaving a thick ridge for the wire. Cut out a petal shape using one of the large rose petal cutters (or use the templates on page 140). I usually make three large and three small petals (although sometimes I only use four petals, depending on the variety of poppy).

and then position the larger ones in-between them. Add an extra 20 or 18-gauge wire to strengthen the stem if required. I prefer to assemble the flower while the petals are still pliable as this makes it easier to re-shape the flower, creating a more realistic shape. Tape over the stem several times with full-width tape to thicken the stem, and then polish it using the side of a pair of scissors.

Buds

10. Bend a hook in the end of a 20 or 18-gauge wire. Mould a ball of Holly/Ivy coloured flower paste into an egg shape. Insert the moistened, hooked wire into the broad end of the shape. Divide the bud into two, three or four sections using either a scalpel or a cutting wheel (again, this will depend which variety of poppy you are making). Next, create a hairy effect using a fine pair of curved scissors. Tape over the stem several times with Nile green floristry tape.

6. Insert a hooked 26 or 24-gauge white wire into the ridge. Vein the petals using the silk veining tool in a fan formation. Frill the curved edge by increasing the pressure with the silk veining tool. Cup the petal and allow to firm up in a former made from a strip of kitchen paper tied into a ring shape. Repeat the process to make the required number of petals.

Colouring and Assembly

7. The colouring will depend on the variety you are making. I have used a mixture of plum, African violet and Edelweiss dusts applied from the base of each petal and fading out towards the edge. Colour both the inside and outside of each petal.

8. Paint extra detail onto the base of each petal using a fine paintbrush and a mixture of Blackberry, Cyclamen and Violet Liquid Food Colours. Over-dust with a patch of aubergine craft dust.

9. Tape the smaller petals around the base of the stamens using half-width Nile green floristry tape,

11. Dust the bud with Forest Green, Holly/Ivy and Edelweiss Dust Food Colours. Add a touch of White Satin Lustre Dust or Magic Sparkle Dust to enhance the hairy finish of the bud. Hold the stem just behind the bud with a pair of pliers, take hold of the end of the wire with your other hand, and firmly bend the stem over.

Leaves

12. Roll out some green flower paste, leaving a thick ridge down the centre. Cut out the leaf shape using the Armenian poppy leaf cutter (or use the templates on page 140). Insert a moistened 26 or 24–gauge wire into the thick ridge. Soften the edges with a metal ball tool. Vein the leaf using the Oriental poppy leaf veiner. The cutter does not match the veiner perfectly, however, an attractive finish can still be obtained. Make extra cuts into the shape if required. Pinch the leaf from the base to the tip. Leave to dry slightly before dusting.

13. Dust in layers with Forest Green, Holly/Ivy, Edelweiss and White Satin Dust Food Colours. Larger groups of foliage may be made either by using the whole veiner shape as a template for the leaf (although this can be a bit tricky), or by taping several groups of foliage together to form a larger leaf shape.

Assembly

14. Tape the leaves behind both the flowers and buds. Add extra leaves down the stem and whenever you join two stems together. Dust the stems with the same mixture as for the buds and foliage.

45

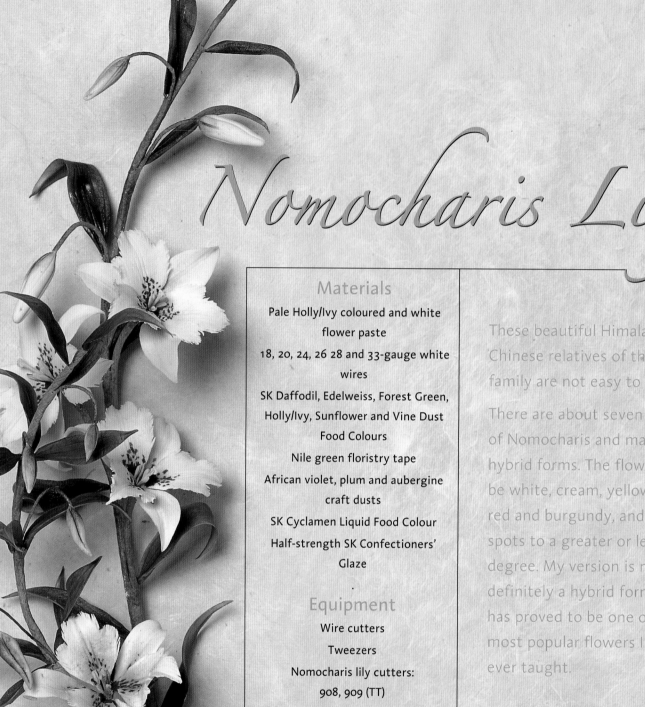

Nomocharis Lily

Materials

Pale Holly/Ivy coloured and white flower paste

18, 20, 24, 26 28 and 33-gauge white wires

SK Daffodil, Edelweiss, Forest Green, Holly/Ivy, Sunflower and Vine Dust Food Colours

Nile green floristry tape

African violet, plum and aubergine craft dusts

SK Cyclamen Liquid Food Colour

Half-strength SK Confectioners' Glaze

Equipment

Wire cutters

Tweezers

Nomocharis lily cutters: 908, 909 (TT)

Plain-edge cutting wheel (PME)

SK Great Impressions Stargazer B Petal Veiner

Metal ball tool (CC)

Fine paintbrush

Dresden tool (Jem) (optional)

These beautiful Himalayan and Chinese relatives of the lily family are not easy to grow.

There are about seven species of Nomocharis and many hybrid forms. The flowers can be white, cream, yellow, pink, red and burgundy, and all have spots to a greater or lesser degree. My version is most definitely a hybrid form and has proved to be one of the most popular flowers I have ever taught.

Pistil

1. Take a small ball of pale green coloured flower paste and work it onto the end of a short length of 33-gauge white wire. Form a small round bead at the end of the wire and then work it down until you have the wire covered with a thin covering of pale green paste. Flatten the bead at the top. Pinch into three sections using tweezers. Dust lightly with Vine Dust Food Colour. There should be a rounded ovary at the base of the pistil. However, I tend to leave it off in most cases as it makes it easier to assemble the stamens into a group.

Stamens

2. Attach a small amount of white paste onto the end of a very short length of 33-gauge wire. Smooth the sides to form an anther. Mark a line down the length of either side using a plain-edge cutting wheel. Repeat to make six stamens. Dust with a mixture of Sunflower and Daffodil Dust Food Colours. Using quarter-width Nile green floristry tape, attach the six stamens around the pistil so that they are slightly shorter than the pistil.

Inner Petals

3. Roll out a piece of white flower paste, leaving a thick ridge for the wire (use a grooved board if you prefer). Cut out the wider petal shape using the cutter (or the template on page 140) and insert a moistened 28-gauge wire into about a third of the length of the petal. Place the petal on a pad and soften the edges with a ball tool, working half on the petal and half on the pad.

4. Vein the petal using the Stargazer B veiner. Add three extra veins to the centre of the petal using the plain-edge cutting wheel; be careful not to apply too much pressure as you might cut through the petal. Create a fringed effect around the edge of the petal using the small wheel of the cutting wheel. Pinch from the base to the tip to accentuate the central veining. Curve the tip back slightly. Repeat to make three inner petals.

Outer Petals

5. Roll out some white flower paste, leaving a thick ridge down the centre. Cut out the petal shape using the plainer of the two cutters in the set (or the template). Insert a moistened 28-gauge white wire into about half the length of the ridge. Soften the edges and vein using the Stargazer B veiner. Pinch the petal from the base to the tip to accentuate the central vein. Curl the tip slightly and then dry slightly before starting the next stage.

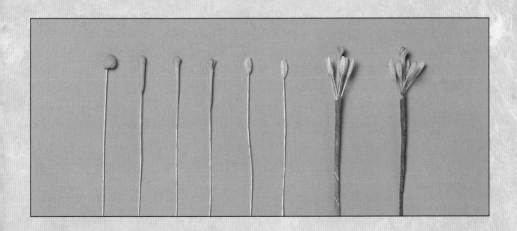

47

Colouring and Assembly

6. The petals may be dusted before or after the flower has been assembled. I tend to assemble the petals first and then add the colour. Tape the three inner petals around the base of the stamens using Nile green floristry tape. Next, position the narrow petals slightly behind the inner three (filling in the gaps). Dust the flower with a light mixture of plum, African violet and Edelweiss dusts. Dust from the base of each petal, fading the colour towards the tips. To create a spotted variety, paint spots onto the petals using a fine brush and Cyclamen Liquid Food Colour. Dust the backs of the flower a darker shade, adding a little aubergine craft dust if required to create more depth. Dust the tips with a light mixture of Vine and Edelweiss Dust Food Colours. Steam the flowers to set the colour and take away the dry, dusted finish.

Buds

7. Take small balls of white flower paste and form them into cones, then roll them into fairly rounded buds. Insert a hooked, moistened 26 or 24-gauge wire into the rounded base of the bud. Mark into thirds using a cage (see page 139) or the plain-edge cutting wheel. Dust the buds in the same way as for the flowers.

Leaves

8. The leaves occur singly, in pairs and sometimes in sets of three. Roll out some pale green coloured paste, leaving a thick ridge for the wire. Cut out a freehand leaf shape using the cutting wheel or a sharp scalpel. Insert a 28 or 26-gauge wire, depending upon the size of the leaf. Soften the edge with a ball tool.

9. Mark a series of fine lines down the leaf using either a Dresden tool or a plain-edge cutting wheel. (Alternatively, you could use a lily leaf veiner.) Dust in layers with Forest Green and Holly/Ivy Dust Food Colours. Catch the edges with a small amount of aubergine craft dust. Allow to dry, then dip in half-strength confectioners' glaze.

Assembly

10. Tape a few smaller leaves on to the end of a 20 or 18-gauge wire. Add a small bud and a set of leaves where they join the stem. Tape tightly with half-width Nile green tape. Work down the stem, increasing the size of both the leaves and the buds. Gradually introduce a flower accompanied by a set of leaves. Add extra wire if required as you work down the stem. Dust the stem with Holly/Ivy and aubergine.

African Corn Lily

Ixia, a flowering bulb native to South Africa, was first cultivated in
the UK in around 1788; since then there have been numerous
cultivars and colour assortments. The flowers are often grown as
hothouse plants, although some varieties will flower outdoors too.
They can also be bought as cut flowers, lasting ten to twelve days
in a vase or arrangement. I have chosen to make *I.viridiflora* an
unusual greenish-blue species flower
with a dramatic dark violet/black eye.
There are also white, cream, pink,
yellow, orange, coral and red varieties.

Materials

White seed head stamens or freesia
stamens
High-tack, non-toxic craft glue
White flower paste
SK Bluegrass, Daffodil, Edelweiss and
Sunflower Dust Food Colours
22, 26, 30 and 33-gauge wires
SK Cyclamen Liquid Food Colour
Nile green floristry tape

Equipment

Nerine/large snowdrop cutter:
470 (TT)
Medium metal ball tool (CC)
CelStick (CC)
Plain-edge cutting wheel (PME)
Fine paintbrush

Pistil (Optional)

1. Cut the tips off both ends of three white stamens. Bond the three stamens together using high-tack glue, leaving the very ends unglued so that you can curl them back slightly. Squeeze the stamens and glue together to reduce the bulk. Allow to dry.

Stamens

2. Cut the tips from three more stamens and attach a slim sausage of white flower paste to one end of each. Colour the tips with Daffodil and Sunflower Dust Food Colours.

3. Using a small amount of high-tack, non-toxic glue, attach the stamens and pistil onto the end of a 26-gauge wire; they all need to be fairly short for the flower, and the pistil should sit below the stamens. Allow to dry.

Flower

4. Roll out some white flower paste, leaving a bump at the centre to add support to the petals. Cut out the petal shape using the large snowdrop/nerine cutter (or see template on page 141). Repeat to make a second layer. Place both layers onto a pad and soften the edges using a metal ball tool; use a rolling action on each petal, working half on the paste and half on the pad. Next, hollow out and cup the length of each petal. Mark a very gentle central vein down each petal.

5. Moisten the centre of one of the layers and place the second layer on top. Position the petals so that they alternate to form an open six-petal shape. Open up the centre a little with the pointed end of a CelStick.

6. Moisten the base of the stamens, and then thread the flower shape onto the wire. Pinch the flower from behind to secure it to the wire at the base of the stamens. Pinch the tips of the petals to give the flower some shape. Allow the flower to dry a little, hanging upside down.

Buds

7. Cut several short lengths of 33 or 30-gauge wire. Roll a small ball of white flower paste, and then form it into a cone shape. Insert a moistened wire into the base of the cone and thin the base down onto the wire a little. Using a plain-edge cutting wheel, divide the bud into three. Repeat to make several buds in graduating sizes.

Dusting and Assembly

8. Colour the flowers and the buds a gentle green-blue colour using a mixture of Bluegrass and Edelweiss Dust Food Colours. Paint a dark eye at the centre of each flower using a fine paintbrush and Cyclamen Liquid Food Colour. Add a patch of Cyclamen at the base of each flower and bud.

9. Tape over each bud and flower stem with half-width Nile green floristry tape. Next, tape the buds onto a 24 or 22-gauge wire, starting with the smallest buds and gradually increasing their size down the stem. Finally, add a few flowers onto the stem. Steam the flowers to set the colour and take away the dry, dusted appearance.

51

This unusual wooden leaf container forms a perfect base to set off the Oriental poppies, Nomocharis lilies and Ixia used in this stylish arrangement.

Oriental Poppy Arrangement

Flowers

3 Oriental poppy flowers

5 Oriental poppy buds

20 Oriental poppy leaves

5 stems of Nomocharis lilies

7 stems of Ixia

Equipment

Nile green floristry tape

18 and 20-gauge wires

Florists' Staysoft

Wire cutters

61cm (24") large wooden leaf container

Pliers

Preparation

1. Strengthen any of the flower stems that may need additional support by taping extra 20 or 18-gauge wires alongside the main stems. Attach a piece of florists' Staysoft offset into the base of the wooden leaf container.

Assembly

2. Bend a hook in the end of each poppy flower and bud stem to provide extra support. Insert the three poppies into the Staysoft, using the largest flower as the focal point. Next, add the stems of poppy buds and foliage to add height, width and shape to the arrangement.

3. Bend a hook in the end of each of the Nomocharis lily stems. Curve the stems slightly as you add them to the arrangement to add further height and shape.

4. Finally, add the stems of aqua coloured Ixias to add extra interest. Use extra poppy leaves to fill in any gaps in the arrangement.

Purple Passion

Delicate sprays of purple Petrea flowers have been used to soften the bold and exotic flowers of Gustavia on this unusual, pretty two-tier wedding cake.

Cake and Decoration

15cm (6") and 25.5cm (10") oval rich fruitcakes

Apricot glaze

1.4kg (3lb) white almond paste

Clear alcohol (e.g. white rum, cherry or orange liqueur)

1.9kg (4lb) white sugarpaste

Small amount of royal icing

3mm fine pale pink ribbon to trim the base of the cakes

15mm decorative pale pink ribbon to trim the board

Equipment

15cm (6") thin oval board

38cm (15") oval cake drum

Non-toxic glue stick

Piping bag

No. 0 piping tube

Fine paintbrushes

Nile green floristry tape

1 medium food-grade posy pick (W)

Flowers and Foliage

2 Gustavia flowers

4 Gustavia buds

10 Gustavia leaves

10 stems of Petrea (various lengths)

10 Calathea leaves

Preparation

1. Place the small oval cake onto a board of the same size. Brush both cakes with apricot glaze, and then cover with white almond paste. Leave to dry overnight. Moisten the surface of the almond paste with clear alcohol and cover with white sugarpaste. Use a pair of sugarpaste smoothers to achieve a smooth, polished finish.

2. Cover the large oval board with white sugarpaste and position the large coated cake on top. Use the smoothers again to join the base of the cake to the board. For a professional finish, polish the surface a little more using a pad of sugarpaste pressed into the palm of your hand. Place the top tier on top of the base tier so that it is offset slightly. Leave to dry.

3. Attach a fine band of pale pink ribbon around the base of each cake using a tiny amount of royal icing to hold it in place. Use a non-toxic glue stick to attach the broader pink ribbon to the edge of the base board.

Side Design

4. Use a piping bag fitted with a No. 0 piping tube and filled with a small amount of white royal icing to pipe an embroidery design onto the cakes. You can either do this freehand or trace and scribe the design (see page 141) onto the cakes first. Start by piping the outline of the petals and leaves, and then carefully soften them by brushing with a slightly damp, fine paintbrush to form a semi-brush embroidered design. Add the dots to form the stamens of the flowers and smaller blossom trails. Pipe the whole design in white royal icing, and then dilute some Dust Food Colours with clear alcohol to colour in the design.

Assembly

5. Tape together two floral sprays as described in Purple Passion Spray on pages 64-65. Insert the smaller spray into a posy pick for the top tier and place the second spray on the board.

Gustavia

There are several species of Gustavia from tropical Central and South America. They are small evergreen trees that are prized for their very large, attractive, fragrant, waxy flowers. They look like they should be related to the magnolia family, but are in fact closer to the Brazil nut tree. They are very extravagant to make as the centre requires four bunches of stamens! Do not let this put you off, as you will only require one or two flowers on a cake to make a dramatic effect. I have scaled the size of the flowers and foliage down a little to make them more suitable for cakes – the foliage can be up to three feet in length! The flowers can be white, creamy-white, pink, coral or mauve tinged.

Materials

18, 22, 24 and 26-gauge white wires

Pale and mid-Holly/Ivy coloured and white flower paste

Cold porcelain (optional)

Four bunches of white seed head stamens

Non-toxic, high-tack craft glue

SK Bulrush, Daffodil, Edelweiss, Forest Green, Holly/Ivy, Sunflower and Vine Dust Food Colours

Aubergine, coral and plum craft dusts

Half-strength SK Confectioners' Glaze

Nile green and brown floristry tape

Kitchen paper

Equipment

Fine-nosed pliers

Fine scissors

Fine angled tweezers

Fine paintbrushes

Large magnolia cutters: 452, 453, 454 (TT)

Petal templates (page 141)

SK Great Impressions Stargazer B Petal Veiner

Large metal ball tool (CC)

Medium fuchsia sepal cutter: 309 (TT)

CelStick (CC)

Plain-edge cutting wheel (PME)

Cattleya orchid wing petal cutters: 3, 6, 9 (TT) (optional)

SK Great Impressions Gardenia Leaf Veiner (very large)

Pistil

1. The pistil is hidden deep in the centre of the stamens. Form a ski-stick shape in the end of a 22-gauge wire using a pair of fine-nosed pliers. Moisten the end of the wire and insert it into a ball of white cold porcelain or flower paste. I generally use a piece of cold porcelain at the centre of the stamens as it is much easier to attach the stamens using a non-toxic craft glue. If you are using flower paste, you may prefer to use a sugar glue mixture of flower paste and egg white (see Important Note on page 133) to attach the stamens to a sugar centre.

2. Mould the ball to create a sharp point at the centre, and then flatten and pinch the edges (it should look rather like a spinning top). Dust the centre with a light mixture of Edelweiss and Vine Dust Food Colours. It is advisable to allow this part to dry for a few hours before attaching the stamens.

Stamens

The stamens are very waxy and curled tightly in a newly opened flower. I have created the centre of a more mature flower, simply because it was easier to replicate.

3. Divide four whole bunches of seed head stamens into smaller groups of around twenty to thirty stamens. Bond the base of each small group together using some non-toxic, high-tack craft glue, or a blended mixture of flower paste and egg white if you are making the centre in sugar. Blend the craft glue or sugar glue into the stamens, flattening them as you work, so that the glue covers around half the length of each group. Leave to set for about five minutes.

4. Trim off the tips of the stamens at the heavily glued end. Curl the remaining tips and part of the length of the stamens using a pair of tweezers. Apply a little more craft glue (or softened flower paste/egg white mix) and attach the stamens around the semi-dried pistil centre. Press them firmly against the sides of the pistil to secure them. You might find that you will need to push each of the groups closer together to create a more compact centre. Continue to add the stamen groups, curling each a little more if required, until you have formed an attractive ring of stamens. Allow the glue (or sugar glue) to dry before the next stage.

5. Create a solid base by adding a strip of white paste around the base of the stamens. Trim away the excess, and then mark a series of fine lines into the paste to represent an extension of the stamens. Leave to dry.

6. Dust the tips of the stamens with a mixture of Daffodil and Sunflower Dust Food Colours. Next, lightly dust the fleshy section at the base with a mixture of Edelweiss, Vine and a touch of Daffodil Dust Food Colours mixed together. Tinge the length of the stamens with a mixture of plum and coral craft dusts.

Petals

The number of petals varies between species of Gustavia. I have used five large and five small to make my hybridised version.

7. The magnolia cutters used for this flower need to be adjusted slightly to make them wider in shape (see templates on page 141). Roll out some white flower paste quite thickly so the petals are fleshy, leaving an even fleshier ridge for the wire. Cut out a petal shape and rub your thumb over the petal edge against the cutter to achieve a clean-cut edge. Insert a moistened 26-gauge wire into the thick ridge of the petal.

8. Soften the edges of the petal using a metal ball tool and a rolling action, working half on the paste and half on your hand or a pad. The edges can be slightly wavy if desired. Vein the petal using the Stargazer B petal veiner.

9. Hollow out the petal using a large ball tool to create a slightly cupped petal shape. Pinch the petal from the base through to the tip. Repeat to make five large and five smaller petals. Some Gustavia petals are more heart shaped at the tips; this can easily be achieved by cutting into the tip of the petals with a sharp pair of scissors. Allow the petals to firm up a little, curving them back to form a very lazy 'S' shape. Tape the petals around the stamen centre before they have had a chance to dry completely, then re-shape the arrangement if necessary to give a more relaxed look to the piece.

Colouring

10. Dust the base of the petals very gently with a light mixture of Vine and Edelweiss Dust Food Colours. Use a light mixture of the plum, coral and Edelweiss dusts used on the stamens earlier to catch the very edges of the petals.

Calyx

11. Roll out some pale green coloured flower paste quite thickly, leaving a thicker section at the centre for support. Cut out the calyx shape using the medium fuchsia sepal cutter (or template). Broaden each of the four sections using a CelStick and a rolling action, keeping a thicker ridge down the centre of each sepal. Moisten the calyx and thread it up onto the back of the flower. Dust lightly with Vine and Edelweiss Dust Food Colours. When the flower is dry, hold it over the steam from a kettle to give it a slight shine and a waxy appearance.

Buds

12. Hook the end of a 22-gauge wire and moisten. Roll a ball of white flower paste and insert the moistened, hooked wire into the base. Leave to dry for a few hours if possible. Next, roll out some white flower paste and cut out five fleshy petals using the smallest of the magnolia petal cutters. Soften the edges and vein using the Stargazer veiner. Moisten the petals and attach them onto the bud in turn: attach them opposite each other to start with, and then position the others to cover the central ball completely. You will need to position them so that the points of the petals join and overlap slightly at the centre. Trim off the excess of each petal from the base of the bud to produce a strong, tight ball-shaped bud. Attach a calyx as for the flower.

13. Dust the base of the bud with a mixture of Vine and Edelweiss Dust Food Colours. Apply some of the flower colour quite strongly onto the tips of the petals. Over-dust with aubergine craft dust. Pass over steam to set the colour.

Leaves

14. Roll out some mid-Holly/Ivy coloured flower paste, leaving a thick ridge for the wire. The leaves are fleshy and can be cut out using either the plain-edge cutting wheel or various sizes of Cattleya orchid wing petal cutters. Insert a 26 or 24-gauge wire into the thick ridge, depending upon the size of the leaf. Soften the edge with a ball tool. Vein the leaf using the large Gardenia leaf veiner. Pinch the leaf from the base to the tip to accentuate the central vein.

15. Dust the leaves before the paste has had a chance to fully dry so that a strong colouring can be achieved. First, dust the edges with a little aubergine craft dust. Next, dust in layers of Forest Green, Holly/Ivy and Vine Dust Food Colours. Allow to dry before dipping each leaf into half-strength confectioners' glaze.

Assembly

16. Tape the buds, flowers and leaves with half-width brown floristry tape onto 18-gauge wires. Thicken the branch as you work with extra layers of tape and shredded lengths of kitchen paper. To add texture to the stem, twist some brown tape back onto itself to form a long strand. Wrap this around the branch in areas where the buds, flowers and leaves are joined to the main branch. Tape over the twisted ridges with more tape to create a more subtle finish. 'Polish' the stems with the side of a pair of scissors. Dust with Bulrush Dust Food Colour. Seal the stem with a light layer of high-tack, non-toxic craft glue. The glue dries clear to leave a shiny surface.

Petrea

There are about thirty species of Petrea. They grow as trees, shrubs and semi-climbing vines, and are mostly native to the Caribbean, Central and South America. At first glance they look like flowers within flowers – they are actually made up from a blossom at the centre of five outer sepals. The flowers may be white, lavender or purple.

Materials

Pale Holly/Ivy coloured and white flower paste

22, 28. 30 and 33-gauge white wires

African violet and deep purple craft dusts

SK Daffodil, Edelweiss, Forest Green, Holly/Ivy and Vine Dust Food Colours

SK Glaze Cleaner (Isopropyl Alcohol)

Nile green floristry tape

Equipment

Small five-petal blossom cutter: 100 (TT)

CelStick (CC)

Fine, sharp scissors

Ceramic silk veining tool (HP)

Single petal daisy cutter: 90 (TT)

Fine pliers

Metal ball tool (CC)

Plain-edge cutting wheel (PME)

SK Great Impressions Briar Rose Leaf Veiner

Simple leaf cutters: 225-232 (TT)

Corolla (Inner Flower)

1. Knead a small amount of white flower paste and roll it into a ball. Next, roll and form it into a teardrop shape. Pinch from the broad end of the teardrop to thin it out, forming a hat shape. Place it onto a non-stick board and roll a CelStick over the paste to thin it out further. Cut out the five-petal blossom shape.

2. Open up the throat of the flower using the pointed end of a CelStick or silk veining tool. Use a fine pair of scissors to make a small 'V' shaped cut from in-between each petal. Next, place the flower over your index finger and broaden and vein each petal slightly using the silk veining tool (one petal should be slightly larger than the others). You might need to re-cut the petals at this stage with scissors if the paste merges back together. Insert a hooked, moistened 30 or 33-gauge wire into the throat of the flower, and neaten the back.

Outer Sepals

3. There are five wired outer sepals for each flower. First of all you will need to make the single petal daisy cutter a little narrower in

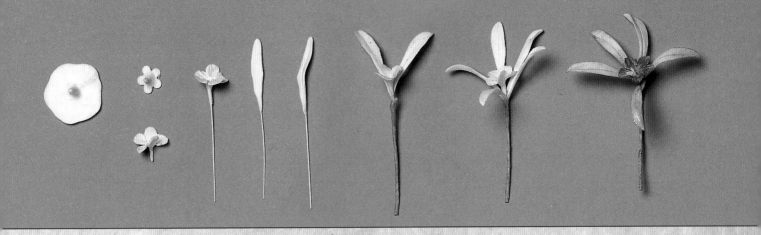

shape by simply squeezing it with a pair of fine pliers. Roll out a small amount of white flower paste, leaving a fine ridge for the wire. Cut out the sepal shape and insert a moistened 33-gauge wire (or 35-gauge if you can get it) into the thick ridge. Soften the edge of the sepal with a ball tool to take away the hard edges. Use the small end of the plain-edge cutting wheel to draw a central vein down the sepal. Pinch a little from the base through to the tip to shape it slightly. Repeat to make five sepals.

Colouring and Assembly

4. You may wish to dust the inner flower and outer sepals before taping them together, but the easiest way is to tape the five wired sepals around the inner flower as you make them and then dust the whole thing at the end. The inner flower is usually darker than the outer sepals. Use a mixture of African violet and deep purple craft dusts mixed with a tiny amount of Edelweiss Dust Food Colour to colour the inner flower. Dust the outer sepals, making sure they appear much paler.

5. Add a touch of Daffodil Dust Food Colour to the centre of the inner flower. The real flower has a white highlight at the centre of the inner flower, but I have chosen to omit it. However, this can be achieved by painting a small patch of Edelweiss Dust Food Colour diluted with clear alcohol onto the largest of the five petals.

Buds

6. Bend a hook in the end of a 33-gauge wire and moisten with glue. Form a ball of white flower paste into a cone shape. Insert the moistened hooked wire into the base of the bud. Thin down the base of the bud onto the wire to

form a finer neck. Divide the bud into five using either a cage with five wires (see page 139) or a plain-edge cutting wheel. Make the buds in graduating sizes. Dust in the same way as the outer sepals of the flower.

Leaves

7. Roll out some pale green flower paste, leaving a thick ridge for the wire (you might prefer to use a grooved board for this). Cut out the leaf shape using a simple leaf cutter or freehand using the plain-edge cutting wheel. Insert a 30 or 28-gauge wire into the leaf, depending on its size. Soften the edge slightly using a metal ball tool. Vein the leaf using the Briar rose leaf veiner. Pinch the leaf from the base to the tip to accentuate the central vein.

8. Dust in layers, starting with a light dusting of Forest Green, fading towards the edges. Over-dust gently with Holly/Ivy and Vine. The leaves are not shiny so will only require a light steaming to set the colour.

Calathea

Materials

Pink flower paste (coloured with SK
Fuchsia Paste Food Colour)

20, 22 and 24-gauge white wires

SK Edelweiss, Forest Green, Holly/Ivy,
Lilac and Vine Dust Food Colours

SK Glaze Cleaner (Isopropyl Alcohol)

Plum craft dust

Half-strength SK Confectioners'
Glaze

Nile green floristry tape

Equipment

Plain-edge cutting wheel (PME)

Leaf template (page 141)

Metal ball tool (CC)

Dresden tool (PME) (optional)

Flat paintbrushes

Stencil brush or toothbrush (new)

Calatheas are attractive, decorative foliage plants from South America. This variety *C. multi tricolour* has variegated green, cream and pink splashed leaves, with a stronger pink underside. Although the plant does produce flowers, they tend to be small and inferior against the highly decorative leaves.

Leaves

1. Roll out some pink coloured flower paste, leaving a thick ridge down the centre for the wire. Cut out the leaf shape using the plain-edge cutting wheel and a Calathea leaf template (page 141) or simply cut out the shape freehand.

2. Insert a moistened 24 or 22-gauge white wire into the thick ridge of the leaf. Place the leaf on a pad with the ridge uppermost, and soften the edges slightly using a medium sized metal ball tool.

3. Create a central vein and some side veining using either the plain-edge cutting wheel or a Dresden veining tool – these veins need to be on the back of the leaf so that they create ridged veining on the front. Turn the leaf over and start to hollow out the area in-between each of the ridged veins using a small to medium sized metal ball tool. This hollowing out process will give the leaf more of its natural character. Pinch the leaf from the base to the tip and allow it to dry fairly flat with a slight curl to the tip. Repeat to make leaves of varying sizes.

Colouring

4. Dust the back of each leaf heavily with plum and Lilac or aubergine craft dust. Paint the front of the leaf in a series of layers, starting with a mid-green mixture of Holly/Ivy and Edelweiss Dust Food Colours diluted with isopropyl alcohol. The markings on the leaves vary in their arrangement.

Use a small, flat brush to create some large streaks and strokes on the leaf. Gradually add some darker markings by adding a touch of Forest Green to the mixture. With a clean brush, add paler streaks on top of the markings using Edelweiss Dust Food Colour mixed with isopropyl alcohol. Try not to be too neat with the painting – you are simply creating an effect.

5. Once the basic markings have been added, use a stencil brush or a clean toothbrush (kept only for craft work) to splash and splatter some fine spots over the leaf. Over-dust each leaf on the upper surface with the various greens to soften the painted effect. A tinge of the plum colouring can be added to the upper surface too. Dip each leaf into half-strength glaze.

Purple Passion Spray

The instructions described here are suitable for both sprays from the Purple Passion wedding cake on page 55. The spray from the bottom tier is slightly larger than the other, even though they both use only a single Gustavia as their focal point.

Flowers and Foliage

5 stems of Petrea

1 Gustavia flower

3 Gustavia buds

5 Gustavia leaves

7 Calathea leaves

Equipment

20 and 22-gauge wires

Nile green floristry tape

Wire cutters

Fine-nosed pliers

Preparation

1. First of all, strengthen the flower and leaf stems by taping a 22 or 20-gauge wire onto them.

Assembly

2. Group three Gustavia buds together alongside the large Gustavia flower. Tape them together using half-width Nile green floristry tape.

3. Next, create the shape of the spray by gradually taping in the five curving stems of Petrea flowers. Bend the base of each stem with pliers against the main Gustavia stem as you add them to give them support in the spray.

4. Fill in the gaps in the spray using both the Gustavia and Calathea foliage. Trim off any excess wire and neaten the handle of the spray with full-width floristry tape.

Daylily Wedding Cake

I have used an unusual combination of late summer flowers, fruit and decorative foliage in this attractive, rich coloured, two-tier design. The strongly coloured Daylily forms the focal point with the chillies, 'red gooseberry vine' and orange Grevillea leaves extending strong, vibrant colours through the rest of the bouquet.

Cake and Decoration

15cm (6") and 25.5cm (10") round
rich fruitcakes

Apricot glaze

1.4kg (3lb) white almond paste

Clear alcohol (e.g. white rum, cherry
or orange liqueur)

1.9kg (4lb) white sugarpaste

Fine peach ribbon to trim the cakes

Small amount royal icing (optional)

Broad peach ribbon to trim the cake
drum

Equipment

15cm (6") round thin cake board

38cm (15") round cake drum

Non-toxic glue stick

Large food-grade posy pick (HW)

Flowers and Foliage

Daylily bouquet (see page 76-77)

Preparation

1. Position the small cake on top of a thin cake board of the same size. Brush both cakes with apricot glaze and cover with a white almond paste. Leave to dry overnight. Moisten the surface of the almond paste with clear alcohol and cover with white sugarpaste. Use a pair of sugarpaste smoothers to achieve a smooth finish.

2. Moisten the cake drum with cooled, boiled water or clear alcohol and cover with white sugarpaste. Smooth over with a round-edged sugarpaste smoother and trim off the excess paste with a sharp knife. Transfer the large cake onto the coated board so that it sits centrally. Blend the sugarpaste at the base of the cake to meet the paste on the board, creating a neat join. Place the smaller cake on top of the base tier, and again blend the two together to form a neat join.

3. Attach a fine band of peach ribbon around the base of both cakes using either a small amount of royal icing or a mixture of sugarpaste and clear alcohol.

4. Wire up the bouquet as described on page 76 to 77. Insert a large food-grade posy pick into the top tier, and then position the handle of the bouquet in it.

Daylily

There are about 30 species of Daylily (*Hemerocollis*) and many hybridised forms. They are native to eastern Asia, although they have become popular garden plants in many other parts of the world. The colour range is vast, making it a wonderful flower for the sugarcrafter's repertoire. As the name implies, the flower only lasts one day!

Materials

24, 26 and 28-gauge white wires

Cream or white and pale Holly/Ivy coloured flower paste

Half-width Nile green and quarter-width white floristry tape

SK Daffodil, Leaf Green, Nasturtium, Sunflower and Vine Dust Food Colours

SK Glaze Cleaner (Isopropyl Alcohol)

Aubergine and ruby craft dusts

Equipment

Wire cutters

Amaryllis petal cutters: 748, 749 (TT)

Medium metal ball tool (CC)

SK Great Impressions Daylily Petal Veiners

Ceramic silk veining tool (HP)

Curved former

Dresden tool (Jem)

Plain-edge cutting wheel (PME)

Stamens and Pistil

1. Cut six short lengths of 28-gauge white wire. Thicken each stem by inserting each wire in turn into a small ball of paste. Work the paste down the wire to create a fine, smooth filament. Alternatively, tape around the wires using quarter-width white floristry tape. Repeat with all six wires. Bend the stamens gently into a very lazy 'S' shape. You may find this easier if you leave the sugar to firm on the wires for about half an hour before bending the stamens into shape. Attach a tiny sausage of paste onto the end of each stamen, using a tiny amount of egg white (see Important Note on page 133) to secure them in place. Allow to dry.

2. Dust the anthers with a mixture of Daffodil and Sunflower Dust Food Colours. Dust the length of the filament with the colour of the flower you are planning to make. I have painted the stamens of the dark flower with a mixture of isopropyl alcohol and Nasturtium, ruby and aubergine dusts.

3. The pistil is basically a longer version of one of the stamens, minus the anther. The tip of the pistil sometimes splits into three sections. Colour in the same way as for the stamens. Tape the six stamens onto the pistil using half-width Nile green tape. Curve the stamens and pistil to follow the same line.

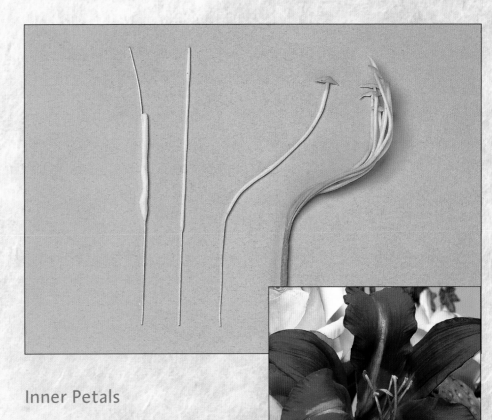

Inner Petals

4. Roll out some flower paste, leaving a thick ridge down the centre for the wire. I generally use cream coloured paste for yellow, orange, red and rust coloured flowers, and white paste for pink and purple forms. Cut out a petal using the wider of the two cutters. Insert a moistened 26-gauge wire into the thick ridge. Soften the edge of the petal using a medium metal ball tool. Vein the petal using the wider petal veiner from the set. Make sure you dust the veiner with plenty of cornflour and don't make the paste too fine as the veiner will stick and cut the paste if you are not careful.

5. Some Daylilies are frilly whilst others have a plainer edge. If required, frill the edges of the inner petals by placing the petal over your index finger and frilling the edge using the ceramic silk veining tool. Pinch the petal from the base to the tip to emphasize the central veining. Allow to firm over a curved former. Repeat to make three inner petals.

Outer Petals

6. The outer petals are made in the same way as the inner three but you will need to use the narrower petal cutter and veiner. Do not frill the edges as much as the inner three.

Colouring and Assembly

7. I generally tape up the flower and then colour the petals; however, you might prefer to colour and then assemble the flower. Tape the three wide inner petals around the stamens using half-width Nile green tape. Add the three narrow petals to fill in the gaps.

8. Dust the base on the inside and heavily on the back of each petal with a mixture of Sunflower and Daffodil Dust Food Colours. Use a mixture of ruby and Nasturtium to colour the main bulk of each petal. To increase the colouring, mix some isopropyl alcohol into the colour and add painted layers on each petal. Allow to dry.

Dust over the top with more of the colour to disguise any streaks left by the painting process. Mix some aubergine craft dust with isopropyl alcohol and add depth to the edges and the centre of each petal. Over-dust with aubergine dust. Steam the flower to set the colour.

9. Add an extra piece of cream coloured paste to the back of the flower to elongate it. Try to blend the paste into the petals as much as you can using the broad end of a Dresden tool. Divide the back into three using a plain-edge cutting wheel.

10. Add an ovary of pale green flower paste at the base of the flower. Divide into three using the cutting wheel. Dust the back of the flower to match the outer surface of the petals using the Sunflower and Daffodil mixture. Dust the ovary with a mixture of Leaf Green and Vine.

Buds

11. Insert a 26 or 24-gauge wire into a cone of cream paste. Thin the broad end of the cone down onto the wire to represent the thin neck of the flower. Divide the bud into three using the cutting wheel. Add a small ovary at the base. Make several buds in graduating sizes. Dust in the same way as for the back of the flower.

'Red Gooseberry Vine'

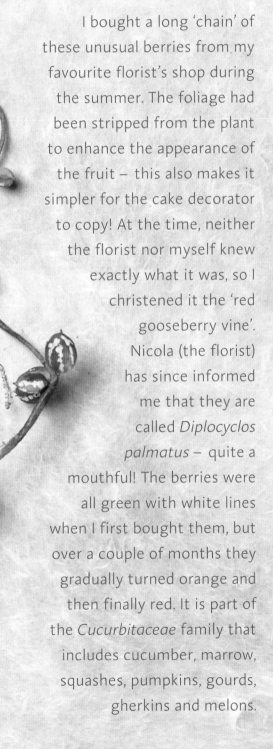

I bought a long 'chain' of these unusual berries from my favourite florist's shop during the summer. The foliage had been stripped from the plant to enhance the appearance of the fruit – this also makes it simpler for the cake decorator to copy! At the time, neither the florist nor myself knew exactly what it was, so I christened it the 'red gooseberry vine'. Nicola (the florist) has since informed me that they are called *Diplocyclos palmatus* – quite a mouthful! The berries were all green with white lines when I first bought them, but over a couple of months they gradually turned orange and then finally red. It is part of the *Cucurbitaceae* family that includes cucumber, marrow, squashes, pumpkins, gourds, gherkins and melons.

Materials

22, 28, 30 and 33-gauge white wires
Half-width Nile green and quarter-width white floristry tape
Pale Holly/Ivy coloured flower paste
Cream and ruby craft dusts
SK Edelweiss, Leaf Green, Holly/Ivy, Poinsettia and Vine Dust Food Colours
SK Glaze Cleaner (Isopropyl Alcohol)
White gouache paint (optional)
Half-strength SK Confectioners' Glaze or edible food spray varnish
36-gauge silk covered reel wire (SWC)
Non-toxic, high-tack craft glue

Equipment

Plain-edge cutting wheel (PME)
Fine paintbrush
Anti-bacterial or baby wipes
Fine-nosed pliers

Dead Flower (Optional)

1. There is often part of the dead flower left on the tip of some of the berries but I generally omit it from the fruit. However, if you wish to create it, simply tape the end of a 30 or 28-gauge wire with quarter-width white floristry tape. The gauge of wire will depend on the size of the fruit you are making. Leave a tiny flap at the end of the wire. Squash and curl the shape slightly to give it a 'dead' appearance. Dust with cream craft dust.

Fruit

2. I usually make the fruit in various sizes using pale green paste, and then dust them to the required ripeness with greens and reds. You might prefer to colour some paste red for the larger fruit. Knead some pale green paste to make it pliable and smooth. Form a smooth ball shape, and then gradually turn it into more of an egg shape.

3. Moisten a wire or the base of a dead flower and thread the wire through the centre of the berry (the point should form the tip of the berry). If you are not using the dead flower technique then simply push the wire through the tip of the fruit so that it only just pierces it. Pinch the base of the fruit onto the wire to secure it into place.

4. Mark about six lines around the fruit from the tip to the base using either a sharp scalpel or plain-edge cutting wheel. Repeat to make fruit in various graduating sizes.

Colouring

5. Dust the fruit accordingly. For the green fruit use a mixture of Vine and Leaf Green Dust Food Colours, use Poinsettia and ruby dusts for the riper red fruit, and a mixture of the two for the in-between stages. To create the white lines you have two options: either mix together some Edelweiss Dust Food Colour with isopropyl alcohol, or use artists' permanent white gouache paint to create stronger lines. The latter method is, of course, not edible, so you must ensure that the paint is kept separate from the cake and any edible materials you have. It is also important to use a different brush for this paint, keeping other brushes for food use only. Dip each berry into half-strength confectioners' glaze or spray with an edible food spray varnish.

Tendrils and Assembly

6. Dip an anti-bacterial wipe into some Vine Dust Food Colour and wipe over a length of 36 or 33-gauge wire to turn it a bright green. Twist the coloured wire around a cocktail stick, modelling tool or the handle of a paintbrush to create tight, springy tendrils. Tape a tendril onto the end of a 22-gauge wire using half-width Nile green floristry tape. Add the fruit singly, in pairs or groups of three. I tend to use the small fruit at the tip of the stem. Continue to add groups of berries with a single tendril until you have created the length of stem required.

7. Dust the stem with Holly/Ivy, Leaf Green and Vine. Seal the stem by rubbing some non-toxic craft glue over the tape. The glue will dry clear and give a slight shine to the stem.

Grevillea Foliage and Chilli Peppers

CHILLIES

Materials

24 and 26-gauge wires

Pale Holly/Ivy and Poinsettia coloured flower paste

SK Forest Green, Holly/Ivy, Leaf Green, Poinsettia, Poppy and Vine Dust Food Colours

Aubergine and ruby craft dusts

SK Confectioners' Glaze

Half-width Nile green floristry tape

Equipment

Angled tweezers

Small ball tool (CC)

GREVILLEA

Materials

Pale Holly/Ivy coloured flower paste

26-gauge wire

SK Berberis, Nasturtium and Poinsettia Dust Food Colours

Half-width Nile green floristry tape

Equipment

Plain-edge cutting wheel (PME)

Scalpel

Chilli peppers and orange dyed Grevillea foliage are both great to use in arrangements and bouquets to add extra interest and a splash of colour.

Chillies

1. Bend a hook in the end of a 26 or 24-gauge wire, depending upon the size of chilli you are making. Form a ball of green or red flower paste into an elongated chilli shape. Insert the hooked moistened wire into the broad end of the chilli and curve the fruit slightly. Make the green chillies slightly smaller in size.

2. To make the calyx, take a small ball of Holly/Ivy coloured flower paste and pinch into a cone. Hollow out the broad end using a small ball tool. Moisten and thread onto the back of the chilli. Thin down the base of the calyx onto the wire. Pinch several ridges around the calyx to represent the sepals.

3. Dust to various degrees of ripeness with Vine, Leaf Green, Poinsettia, ruby and touches of aubergine. Dust the calyx with a mix of Holly/Ivy and Forest Green. Dip the chilli into a full-strength confectioners' glaze, avoiding the calyx. Dip again if required.

4. Tape down the stem with half-width Nile green floristry tape.

Grevillea

1. Roll out some pale Holly/Ivy coloured flower paste, leaving a thick ridge down the centre. Cut out a long, slender leaf shape using the plain-edge cutting wheel. Insert a moistened 26-gauge wire into the thick ridge.

2. Create a jagged edge on the leaf by cutting into it and flicking away from the main body of the leaf with a sharp scalpel.

3. Draw down a central vein using the plain-edge cutting wheel. Pinch to emphasize the central vein.

4. Dust with Berberis, Nasturtium and Poinsettia Dust Food Colours. Tape down the stem with half-width Nile green floristry tape.

Ivy

Ivy is often used to symbolize fidelity, making it ideal foliage for wedding cakes! There are many different ivy cutters and veiners available on the market, allowing the sugarcrafter to create different types very easily. I have used fairly small ivy leaves in this book. However, the method is the same for most varieties.

Materials

Pale or mid-Holly/Ivy coloured flower paste

20, 22, 24, 26, 28, 30 and 33-gauge white wires

Quarter-width Nile green and half-width brown or beige floristry tape

SK Forest Green and Holly/Ivy Dust Food Colours

Aubergine craft dust

Half-strength SK Confectioners' Glaze

Equipment

African ivy cutters (Jem)

Metal ball tool (CC)

SK Great Impressions Birdsfoot Ivy Veiners

Scriber or scalpel

CelStick (CC)

Leaves

1. Roll out some green flower paste, leaving a thick central ridge for the wire (or use a grooved board if you wish). Cut out a leaf shape using one of the four sizes of African ivy cutters.

2. Insert a moistened wire into the central ridge of the leaf. The gauge of wire will depend upon the size of the leaf. Soften the edge with a ball tool.

3. Vein the leaf using a birdsfoot ivy veiner. There are several sizes so choose one that is closest to the leaf you are making.

4. Repeat to make the required number of leaves. Tape over each stem with quarter-width Nile green floristry tape.

Colouring

5. Add depth to each leaf using Forest Green Dust Food Colour. Fade the colour out towards the edges. Be very careful not to add too much colour as it can make the foliage look too blue. Over-dust heavily with Holly/Ivy Dust Food Colour. Add tinges of aubergine craft dust to the edges if desired. Allow to dry.

6. Dip the leaf into half-strength confectioners' glaze, shake off the excess and allow to dry. If you have time and patience then you can etch away the veins on each leaf to create the paler markings that many ivy leaves have. Etch into the glaze and the sugar to create stronger main veins with finer side veining.

Assembly

7. Tape over the end of a 24-gauge wire with half-width brown or beige floristry tape. Curl the end around a CelStick to form a tendril. This part of the stem would usually be new leaves beginning to form, but it is easier to create a tendril. Start adding the smaller leaves down the stem, gradually increasing the size as you work up the stem. Add an extra 22 or 20-gauge wire if needed to create very long trails of ivy.

Daylily Bouquet

Flowers and Foliage

1 Daylily, plus buds

4 apricot tinged roses (see page 81)

3 green lotus pods (see page 17)

5 Croton leaves

12 mixed red and green chilli peppers

1 trailing stem of 'red gooseberry vine'

7 stems of ivy

9 orange Grevillea leaves

3 stems of Tillandsia moss (see page 127)

Equipment

18 and 20-gauge wires

Nile green floristry tape

Fine-nosed pliers

Wire cutters

Preparation

1. If necessary, strengthen and elongate the flowers, foliage and seed head stems by taping them alongside either 20 or 18-gauge wires with half-width Nile green floristry tape.

Assembly

2. Using the Daylily as the focal point, start to tape in the roses grouped in a line on the left hand side. You may use half or even full-width tape to hold them in position. Next, add the lotus pods on the right hand side so that they help to frame the lily. Fine-nosed pliers are useful for bending the stems to group the flowers tightly together. Trim off some of the excess wires as you work using wire cutters.

3. Add the Croton foliage around the edges of the roses and lotus pods. Fill in some of the gaps with small groups of chillies. Tape in a trailing stem of 'red gooseberry vine' to add some length to the bouquet.

4. Create extra length and height by adding some trails of ivy. Finally, add the orange Grevillea foliage and Tillandsia moss to fill in the gaps and add extra interest. Trim off some of the excess wires and tape over the handle of the bouquet with full-width floristry tape to neaten it.

The trend for hand-tied bouquets is fading out, with more brides opting for a more contemporary twist to the traditional wired bridal bouquet. Here, I have used the flowers and seed heads in blocks of colour, but an attractive trailing effect is still retained.

Jaime's Summer Cake

This stunning, brightly coloured three-tier wedding cake was made to celebrate the wedding of Jaime and David Maccoy.

Cake and Decoration

15cm (6"), 20.5cm (8") and 25.5cm (10")
teardrop shaped polystyrene dummy
cakes or rich fruitcakes

2.3kg (5lb) white almond paste (if
using fruitcakes)

Apricot glaze

Clear alcohol (e.g. white rum, cherry or
orange liqueur)

1.6g (3^1/$_2$lb) white sugarpaste mixed
with 1.6g (3^1/$_2$lb) champagne
sugarpaste

Broad magenta ribbon to trim the
boards

Silver paper-covered wire

Fine magenta crimped wire

Assorted glass and plastic beads

Food-grade posy picks (if using
fruitcakes)

Equipment

20.5cm (8"), 25.5cm (10")
and 35.5cm (14") oval cake drums

Piping bag

No. 42 piping tube

Non-toxic glue stick

70cm (27^1/$_2$") large decorative silver
candleholder

Tilting cake stands (CC)

Non-slip mat or double-sided tape

Flowers and Foliage

Top bouquet:

1 full rose

6 rosebuds

4 half roses

6 stems of grape vine

3 stems of sweet pea

3 trailing stems of bougainvillea

Bottom tier bouquet:

Jaime's bouquet, see page (92-93)

Smaller sprays:

4 half roses

12 grape vine leaves

5 sprigs of bougainvillea

Preparation

1. I used sugarpaste-covered polystyrene dummy cakes for this three-tier wedding cake, and then provided the guests at the wedding with individual wrapped slices of rich fruitcake. Real cakes could have been used for the display. However, I prefer to use dummy cakes, as they are much lighter and eliminate the worry of displaying cakes on tilted stands. If you do decide to use real cakes, please refer to Coating a Cake on page 137. Moisten the surface of the boards with clear alcohol and cover them with sugarpaste.

2. Pipe a shell border around the base of each cake using some sugarpaste softened with clear alcohol (such as cherry or orange liqueur for added flavour) and a no. 42 piping tube.

Attach a band of deep magenta ribbon around the edge of the boards using a non-toxic glue stick.

Assembly

3. To make the bouquet for the bottom tier, follow the instructions for Jaime's bouquet (see pages 92 to 93). Wire together a large bouquet for the top of the candleholder and two smaller sprays of flowers. Attach the large bouquet onto the top of the silver candleholder using some of the paper-covered wire. You will need to pull some wire through the bouquet from the front to the back to help hold it in position.

4. Next, add trails of silver paper-covered wire to hang below the bouquet. Curl the ends of the wire to add a touch of detail below the spray. Add lengths of magenta crimped wire with a mixture of

glass and plastic beads threaded onto them. You will need to thread the beads and then twist the wire either side of the bead to hold it in place. These lengths of beaded wire are then entangled into the bouquet, with some hanging below the bouquet and wrapped around the silver paper-covered wire.

5. I find it best to set up the rest of the wedding cake before positioning the other sprays of flowers so that a more balanced effect can be achieved. Use two sizes of clear acrylic tilting cake stands to display the two smaller cakes. I have customized this stand by cutting the base in half, allowing me to use the two stand heights in various positions. The cakes can be held in position using either double-sided tape or a piece of non-slip mat placed in between the cake board and the stand.

6. Insert the handle of each spray directly into the polystyrene dummy cakes. If you are using real cakes then you will need to insert a food-grade plastic posy pick into each cake to hold the flowers in place. Finally, add extra curls of silver paper-covered wire and lengths of beaded magenta crimped wire to each of the sprays to complete the design.

Rose

The Rose (*Rosa*) is the most popular of all bridal flowers. A sugarcraft book would not be complete without one, so here it is! The flower described here has individually wired outer petals that give it some movement, making it easier to use in bouquets and arrangements.

Materials

Mid-Holly/Ivy coloured and white flower paste

18, 26 and 28-gauge white wires

Aubergine, fuchsia, plum and ruby craft dusts

Nile green floristry tape

SK Daffodil, Edelweiss, Forest Green, Holly/Ivy, Leaf Green, Sunflower and Vine Dust Food Colours

Half or quarter-strength SK Confectioners' Glaze

Equipment

Diamond Jubilee rose or large rose petal cutters: 776-778 or 549-551 (TT)

Medium ball tool (CC)

SK Great Impressions Large Rose Petal Veiner

Cupped former or kitchen paper

Rose calyx cutters: nos. R11b, R11c (OP)

CelStick (CC)

Rose leaf cutters (Jem)

SK Great Impressions Briar Rose Leaf Veiner (large)

Rose Cone

1. I have used the very large Diamond Jubilee rose petal cutters for the rose illustrated. However, the instructions below can be used with any rose petal cutters. The important thing to remember is that for a full rose you will need to use two sizes of rose petal cutter. The size of the central cone that the rose is formed around should

measure about two thirds the length of the cutter you plan to use.

Roll a ball of white flower paste into a cone with a sharp point and quite a broad base. Bend a large open hook in the end of an 18-gauge wire. Moisten the hook and insert it into the base of the cone so that it pushes close to the tip of the shape. Pinch a little of the paste from the base of the cone down onto the wire to secure it in place. Leave to dry for at least a few hours, or ideally overnight.

2. Colour a large amount of paste the desired colour (I have used plum craft dust). It is advisable to start with the paste much paler than the finished flower will be and change its colour by applying layers of dust colour afterwards.

Petals

3. For the first and second layers, roll out some paste thinly and cut out four petals using the smaller of the two cutters you are planning to use for the flower. Place the petals on a pad and soften the edges using a medium-sized metal ball tool, but do not frill the edges. Although these inner petals are wrapped tightly around the cone, and not viewed in detail, it is a good idea to place them in turn into the rose petal veiner to give them a little texture.

4. Moisten the centre of one of the petals and place it against a dried wired cone, leaving at least a quarter in of the petal above the tip of the cone. This first petal needs to be tucked tightly from the left hand side into the cone to hide the tip of the cone completely. Wrap the other side of the petal around to form a tight spiral, leaving the end slightly open to take the next petal. Concentrate

on the formation at the top of the bud at this stage – do not worry about covering the base of the cone unless you are making rosebuds.

5. Moisten the base of each of the remaining three petals. Tuck the first one underneath the open edge of the spiral petal on the cone. Place the next petal over the join in the first two, and place the last one of this layer over the join and under the open flap of the first petal to form a spiral. Pull down the petals as you position them to keep the rose centre tight and smooth at this stage. The important thing is to try to get the petals evenly spaced. Keep one of the edges open at this stage so that the first petal of the next layer of three can be tucked underneath.

6. To make the third and fourth layers, roll out some more paste and cut out three more petals using the same sized cutter as before. Soften the edges of the

petals and vein using the rose veiner. Moisten the base of each of the petals. Tuck the first of these three under the open petal from the previous layer. Close the open petal down over it to end the previous layer and start the layer you are working on. Next, add the second petal over the join, and the third slightly over it, but tucked underneath the open edge of the first petal of this layer. The spiral shape continues as before. Keep the edge of the last petal open to take the first petal of the fourth layer.

7. Cut out three more rose petals using the same sized cutter. Repeat the method for the previous layer to complete what will be the fourth layer. The rose can start to open up a little at this stage so do not tighten the petals too much against the previous layer. Depending on the appearance of the rose at this stage, you may wish add another layer of three petals using the same sized cutter.

8. For the fifth layer of petals, roll out some more flower paste. Cut out three more petals using the slightly larger petal cutter. Soften and vein each of the petals as before. Cup the centre of each petal using the ball tool.

9. Moisten the base of each petal. Position the first petal underneath the last petal of the previous layer (or very close to it). Add the next two petals in the same way as before. The rose should be quite open at this stage representing a half-open rose.

10. I usually wire each of the petals individually for the last layer as it gives the rose much more movement. Roll out some paste leaving a thicker ridge at the centre.

Cut out a petal shape using the same sized cutter as used in the previous step. Hook and moisten the end of a 26-gauge wire. Insert the hooked end into the base of the thick ridge. Pinch the petal firmly onto the wire to secure it. Soften the edge of the petal and vein as before. Hollow out the centre of the petal using a ball tool or by rubbing your thumb against the petal.

11. Dry the petal in a cupped former. Alternatively, take a wide strip of kitchen paper and twist it against itself, then tie it into a loop big enough to take a petal. I find these open loops allow the petal to 'breathe' and dry faster. Repeat to make eight to ten petals. Curl back the left and right edges as you go, forming an almost triangular shape.

Assembly and Colouring

12. The rose can be dusted before or after it has been assembled; it very much depends on the depth of colour you are trying to achieve. It is easier to achieve lighter colouring once the rose has been assembled. Tape three petals around the half rose using half-width Nile green floristry tape. Continue to add the remaining petals, positioning them over joins as you go. You will need between eight and ten petals for a full rose.

13. Mix together some Daffodil, Sunflower and Edelweiss Dust Food Colours. Carefully dust the base of each petal on the back and front where you can to add a glow to the rose. For the rest of the rose, I have used a mixture of fuchsia and plum craft dusts. Aim to colour the centre of the rose first as this needs to be stronger than the colouring on the rest of the rose to create a focal point. Dust the remaining petals from the edges towards the centre. Add a little aubergine craft dust to the bright pink mixture and add extra depth of colour to the centre of the rose. Catch the edges here and there if required to balance the colour. Steam the flower and re-dust if a stronger finish is required.

Calyx

14. Roll a ball of Holly/Ivy coloured flower paste into a cone shape. Pinch the base to form a hat shape. Roll out the base to make it a little thinner, although the end result should be rather fleshy. Cut out a calyx shape slightly smaller than required, then re-roll each sepal to create a more elegant, elongated shape. Open up the centre of the calyx using the pointed end of a CelStick. Hollow out the inside of each of the sepals using a ball tool or the rounded end of a CelStick. Pinch each of the sepals to create a subtle ridge on the outside of the calyx. Pinch the tips into a sharp point.

15. Dust the inside of the calyx a slightly paler colour using a light mixture of Edelweiss and Holly/Ivy Dust Food Colours. Using a fine pair of sharp, curved

and Holly/Ivy Dust Food Colours. You may wish to catch the tips of each sepal with a mixture of aubergine and ruby craft dusts.

Leaves

17. The leaves can be in sets of three or five, depending upon the variety of the rose. The first leaf needs to be larger than the others. Roll out some mid-green coloured flower paste, leaving a thick ridge down the centre for the wire. Cut out a leaf shape using your chosen cutter. Insert a moistened 26 or 28-gauge wire into the leaf, depending on the size of the leaf. Soften the edges slightly but do not frill. Vein the leaf in the Briar rose leaf veiner. I use this large veiner for all sizes of rose leaf; if you are making small leaves then simply use the very top part of the veiner to create finer veins. Pinch the leaf from the base to the tip to accentuate the central vein. Repeat to make the required number of leaves in various sizes.

Assembly and Colouring

18. I would recommend taping the leaves into groups before dusting them to achieve a more pleasing balance of colour. Tape two medium sized leaves either side of the larger leaf. Keep each wire very short to the main stem. Add two of the smallest leaves to complete a set. Dust the edges of the leaves with a mixture of plum and aubergine or ruby and aubergine. Add more colour to the right hand side of the leaf and apply some colour to the back of each leaf. Use Forest Green Dust Food Colour to create depth on the upper surface of the leaf. Over-dust with Holly/Ivy, Vine or Leaf Green. Dust the back of the leaves with Edelweiss Dust Food Colour (I use the brush used for the green colours to achieve a pale green effect). Allow the leaves to dry. Dip into a quarter or half-strength confectioners' glaze, shake off the excess and allow to dry. When dusting the leaves, bear in mind that the colour of rose leaves varies between varieties.

scissors, create a series of fine hairs on the edge of each sepal (the number of cuts will depend on the variety of the rose you are making). Moisten the centre of the calyx and thread it up onto the back of the rose. Try to position the sepals over a join in the rose petals. On a fully open rose the sepals fall away from the flower – however, this can make wiring the flower into a spray difficult. It is often best to attach the calyx just before the flowers are taped up so that the soft calyx can move around against the other flowers in the spray.

16. Dust the outside of the calyx with a mixture of Forest Green

Grape Vine Leaves

Grape vine leaves (*Vitis*) make an interesting alternative to ivy in bouquets or arrangements. The leaves can be large, making them ideal for filling space quickly and efficiently. The colouring can be a fresh green or a darker green tinged with reds and aubergine.

Materials

Pale Holly/Ivy coloured flower paste
22, 24 and 26-gauge white wires
SK Forest Green, Holly/Ivy and Vine Dust Food Colours
Aubergine and plum craft dusts
Nile green floristry tape

Equipment

Grape Vine leaf cutters (Jem)
Medium metal ball tool (CC)
SK Great Impressions Grape Vine Leaf Veiners

Leaves

1. Roll out some pale green flower paste, leaving a thick ridge down the centre. Cut out a leaf shape using one of the four sizes of grape vine leaf cutters. You will need to make the larger leaves slightly fleshy to allow for the heavy veining of the grape vine veiners.

2. Hold the thick ridge of the leaf firmly between your finger and thumb, and then gradually insert a moistened 26 or 24-gauge white wire (depending on the size of the leaf). It is easier to insert the wire into the ridge if you hold the wire very close to the end that goes into the ridge. Aim to push the wire into about a quarter to half the length of the leaf.

3. Place the leaf onto a firm foam pad and soften the edge using a medium-sized metal ball tool, holding the tool half on the edge of the leaf and half on the pad. Use a rolling action with the ball tool to give a softened, non-frilly finish.

4. Dust the grape vine veiner with cornflour (especially if it is brand new). Place the leaf into the veiner, carefully lining up the tips of the leaf shape with the central veining of the veiner. Press the two sides of the veiner together firmly, but not so hard that the veins cut through the leaf. Remove the leaf from the veiner and pinch from the base of the leaf to the tip of each section to emphasize the heavier central veining of the leaf. Allow to firm up a little before dusting with colour. Repeat to make leaves in all sizes.

Colouring and Assembly

5. Dust in layers with Forest Green Dust Food Colour, fading the colour towards the edges. Over-dust heavily with Vine and Holly/Ivy Dust Food Colours. Catch the edges with a mixture of plum and aubergine craft dusts. Allow to dry, then dip each leaf into quarter-strength confectioners' glaze.

6. Start a trailing stem of the vine by taping a small leaf onto the end of a 22-gauge wire with half-width Nile green floristry tape. Alternate the leaves down the stem, graduating the sizes as you go. Tendrils may also be added at leaf axils if you wish – these are made simply by wrapping and twisting some 33-gauge wire around the end of a fine paintbrush. Dust the leaves with Holly/Ivy and Vine Dust Food Colours and add tinges of aubergine craft dust.

Bougainvillea

There are about eighteen species of bougainvillea, with many more hybrid varieties. The plants are native to the tropics. The coloured bracts, which at first glance look like petals, can be white, cream, lemon, yellow, orange, rust, pink, magenta, red, purple and aubergine. Some plants even have multi-coloured bracts. The flowers are inferior to the bracts, and are often mistaken for stamens. The foliage of the plant can be plain or variegated.

Materials

Pale Holly/Ivy coloured and white flower paste

20, 22, 24, 26, 28, 30 and 33-gauge white wires

Fine white stamens (optional)

SK Daffodil, Edelweiss, Forest Green, Holly/Ivy, Lilac and Vine Dust Food Colours

Aubergine, fuchsia and tangerine craft dusts

Half-strength SK Confectioners' Glaze

Nile green floristry tape

Equipment

Fine angled tweezers

Tiny plunger blossom cutter (PME)

Dresden tool (Jem)

CelStick (CC)

Bougainvillea cutters (Jem)

Metal ball tool (CC)

SK Great Impressions Bougainvillea Bract Veiner

Simple leaf cutters: 225-232 (TT)

Plain-edge cutting wheel (PME)

SK Great Impressions Briar Rose Leaf Veiner

Buds

1. There are three flowers, buds or a mixture of the two at the centre of the three coloured bracts. To make the buds, work a small piece of white flower paste onto a short length of 33 or 30-gauge wire. The base of the thin buds should be slightly more bulbous than the tip. Pinch a series of ridges onto the sides using angled tweezers. Flatten the tip slightly, and then twist to give it some movement.

Flowers

2. The flowers start off in the same way as the buds, however, no twists are needed. Instead, roll out some white paste thinly and cut out a tiny plunger blossom shape. Double frill the edges of the blossom using the broad end of the Dresden tool, pulling the paste down against the board. Moisten the tip of the prepared bud, and attach the blossom on top. Use the pointed end of a CelStick to secure the blossom and open up the throat. There are stamens in the flowers, but I find that they look better without as the flowers are so small. Leave to dry.

Bracts

3. These leaves or modified bracts need to be made very fine (hence the plant's common name, paper flower). Roll out the white flower paste thinly, leaving a fine ridge to take a 33 or 30-gauge white wire. Cut out a bract shape using one of the two sizes of bougainvillea cutters. Insert a fine wire into the central ridge. Soften the edge using a metal ball tool. Vein the bract with the double-sided bougainvillea bract/petal veiner. Pinch the bract from the base to the tip. Repeat to make three evenly sized bracts for each group of bougainvillea.

Colouring

4. If possible, dust and assemble the flowers and bracts before they are dry – this will help to achieve brighter, stronger colouring and allow you to re-shape the

bracts to create a natural shape. Dust the flowers with a light mixture of Daffodil and Edelweiss Dust Food Colours. Dust the back of each flower and bud with a little of the flower colour and aubergine craft dust or Lilac Dust Food Colour.

5. The flowers actually appear from each bract. In this version I have simplified the formation by grouping the three flowers/buds together, and then positioning and taping three bracts around them. Dust the bracts in varying combinations with tangerine and touches of fuchsia craft dusts. Dust a little Holly/Ivy at the base of the bracts, and occasionally add a touch at the tip. Repeat this process using the smaller cutter to create sets of three, but this time add only three buds at the centre of each group. You will need to make lots of groups of bracts to create impact within the spray.

Leaves

6. Roll out some pale green flower paste, again leaving a narrow ridge for the wire. Cut out the leaf shape using a simple leaf cutter or freehand using the plain-edge cutting wheel. Insert a 30, 28 or 26-gauge wire into the leaf, depending on its size. Soften the edge with a ball tool and vein using either the bougainvillea bract veiner or the Briar rose leaf veiner. Pinch the leaf from the base to the tip to emphasize the central vein.

Dust with Forest Green, Holly/Ivy and Vine Dust Food Colours. Leave to dry. Glaze using half-strength confectioners' glaze.

Assembly

7. Tape the bracts and foliage onto 24, 22 and leading onto 20-gauge wire for larger trailing stems. Start off with the smaller sets of bracts, adding a single leaf where they join the main stem. Gradually introduce the larger sets of bracts. Dust the stems with Holly/Ivy Dust Food Colour. Steam the bracts above a kettle to take away the dry finish left by the dust.

Sweet Pea

Sweet peas were one of the very first flowers I was shown how to make in sugar. This method is a little more time-consuming than the conventional method as the petals are all individually wired, however, the flowers produced are stronger and have more movement to them.

Materials

Mid-Holly/Ivy coloured and white flower paste

20, 24, 26, 28 and 30-gauge white wires

Quarter-strength SK Confectioners' Glaze

SK Daffodil, Edelweiss, Forest Green, Holly/Ivy and Vine Dust Food Colours

Plum craft dust

Nile green floristry tape

Equipment

Sharp scalpel

Plain-edge cutting wheel (PME)

Rose petal cutters: 278, 279, 280 (TT)

Ceramic silk veining tool (HP)

Small CelStick (CC)

Small Briar rose calyx cutter: no. R13 (OP)

Dresden tool (Jem)

Sweet pea cutters: 737, 738 (TT)

Frilling needle or cocktail stick

Fresh sweet pea foliage or SK Great Impressions Peony Leaf Veiner

Fine pliers

Centre or 'Keel'

1. Roll a ball of white flower paste into a teardrop shape. Flatten the shape with your fingers to form a pasty shape. Moisten a hooked 24-gauge wire and insert it into the base of the bud. Pinch a sharp edge on the rounded part of the shape.

2. Using a sharp scalpel or the plain-edge cutting wheel, indent and open up the straight edge to represent the opening where the stamens pop through in the real flower. You will need to make a keel for the centre of each flower and bud. The keel should be slightly smaller in the buds.

Buds

3. Roll out some white flower paste thinly and cut out two rose petal shapes. Cut out a narrow 'V' shape from the rounded edge of one of the petals – this is to represent the two partly formed inner wing petals. Frill both sections of the petal using a silk veining tool. Moisten the pointed base of the shape and attach this onto the back of the keel. Frill the second rose petal in a fan formation using the silk veining tool. Draw down a central vein and attach the petal on top of the split wing petals. Pinch the whole bud together at the base to secure the petals and then curl back the outer petal a little.

Calyx

4. Take a small ball of mid-Holly/Ivy flower paste and form it into a teardrop shape. Pinch out the base to form a small pedicel. Place the shape flat side down on the board and thin out the paste using a small CelStick. Cut out the calyx using the small rose calyx cutter. Elongate each of the sepals a little before hollowing out the back of each with the broad end of a Dresden tool. Open up the centre of the calyx using the pointed end of a CelStick. Moisten the centre and thread onto the back of the bud. Try to position two of the petals on the back of the outer petal. Pinch and curl the tips slightly.

Wing Petals

5. Roll out some white flower paste, leaving a slightly thicker area down the centre (this should measure about half the length of the wing petal cutter). Cut out the petal shape using the cutter. Hook and moisten the end of a 28-gauge wire and insert it into the thicker area at the base of the petal. Pinch the petal on to the wire to make sure it is secure.

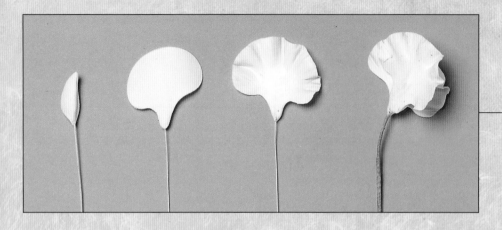

6. Vein and frill the petal in a fan formation on both sides using the silk veining tool. The frill can be softened slightly if necessary using a cocktail stick or frilling needle. Repeat the process to make left and right wing petals. Allow the petals to firm up a little before taping them onto either side of one of the larger keels. I prefer to assemble the flower while the paste is still slightly pliable to achieve a more realistic effect.

Standard Petal

7. Roll out some more white flower paste, again leaving a thick ridge for the wire. Cut out the petal using the larger cutter in the set. Insert a hooked, moistened 28-gauge wire into the base of the ridge.

8. Vein the petals using the ceramic silk veining tool in a fan formation, keeping the point of the tool pointing towards the point of the petal. Next, using the same tool, increase the pressure on the edge to frill it. You might prefer to place the petal over your index finger to frill it.

9. Place the petal on a pad and draw a central vein down the upper side of the petal using the fine end of the Dresden tool. Turn it over on the pad and indent the paste on either side at the base of the petal using the broad end of the Dresden tool. This will create two bumps on the front of the petal, which helps the petal sit comfortably around the wing petals. Allow the petal to firm up slightly before taping it onto the other parts of the flower.

Assembly and Colouring

10. Tape the two wing petals tightly onto either side of the keel using half-width Nile green floristry tape. Position and tape the standard petal behind the wing petals. Again, it helps if the petals are still pliable at this stage so that you can re-shape and curl back the petals if necessary. Allow the flowers to dry a little more before dusting.

11. Mix a small amount of Edelweiss, Daffodil and Vine Dust Food Colours together. Dust the tip of

bracts. Cut several short lengths of 30-gauge wire. Roll a small teardrop piece of mid-green flower paste. Insert a dry wire into the broad end of the teardrop and flatten the paste using the smooth side of a silicone rubber veiner. Pinch the bract from the base through to the tip to shape it a little. Leave to dry.

Tendrils

 The tendrils grow from the leaf stems rather than the flower stems and are good to use because they add instant character to a display. Use quarter-width Nile green tape twisted back on itself to form a fine strand. You will need three tendrils to form one group. Tape the three tendrils together onto a 26-gauge wire, then add another few tendrils below the top set on some of the tendrils.

Assembly

 Tape the flowers and buds into stems with three or four flowers/buds on them. Use a 20-gauge wire to form the main stem and leave a short length of each individual flower stem showing.

the keel and the base of each petal. Use this light green mixture to dust the buds gently.

 Dust the petals with your chosen colour – in this instance I used a mixture of plum craft dust and Edelweiss Dust Food Colour. Dust the back of the standard petal with a flush of the pale green mixture. Attach a calyx as for the bud. Dust the calyx with a mixture of Holly/Ivy and Vine Dust Food Colours.

Leaves

I only usually include the foliage when using sweet peas in a natural style of arrangement.

 Roll out some mid-green flower paste, leaving a central ridge (you might prefer to use a grooved board). Cut out the leaves freehand using a plain-edge cutting wheel. Insert a moistened 28-gauge wire into about half the length of the leaf. Vein the leaf using a suitable veiner (I used a peony leaf veiner on the leaves pictured).

 Some varieties of sweet pea have quite frilly edges others are flat, so decide which you prefer and frill the edges with a ball tool if required. Pinch the leaf to emphasize the central vein. You will need to make the leaves in pairs.

 Dust the leaves using layers of Forest Green, Holly/Ivy, Vine and Edelweiss Dust Food Colours. The leaves are not shiny in nature, so you can either steam them to set the colour or dip them into quarter-strength confectioners' glaze.

Bracts

 At the base of each of the leaf stems, where they join the main stem, there are two small, leafy

Jaime's Bouquet

Flowers and Foliage

3 rosebuds

3 half roses

2 full wired roses

3 stems of sweet pea

5 stems of grape vine leaves

3 stems of bougainvillea

Equipment

18, 20 and 22-gauge wires

Nile green floristry tape

Silver paper-covered wire

Deep magenta crimped wire

Assorted glass and plastic beads

Fine pliers

Wire cutters

Preparation

1. First of all, strengthen any of the flower and foliage stems, if needed, by taping on an additional 18, 20 or 22-gauge wire alongside the main stem. The size of wire used will depend on the size and weight of the flower.

Assembly

2. This semi-crescent bouquet is longer on one side than the other. Take a length of grape vine and bend the end of the wire to a 90° angle. Bend and add another length of vine leaves and tape together using half-width Nile green floristry tape. This will form the length and basic outline of the bouquet. Add a few shorter lengths of vine leaves in the same way to define the shape a little more.

3. Next, add a large rose to the centre of the bouquet to form the focal point. Add the other roses and buds to surround the focal point.

4. Add a few stems of pale pink sweet peas to emphasize the crescent shape of the bouquet. At this stage, I usually start taping up the stems with full-width tape so that all the flowers and foliage are held firmly together.

5. Add and tape in the stems of bougainvillea to fill in the gaps and give some added interest. Add some extra stems of vine leaves at this stage. I have used lengths of silver paper-covered wire to weave through the bouquet and also create some extra curls. Deep magenta crimped wire with beads threaded onto it has also been used to tangle and weave through the flowers and foliage.

This is the bouquet from the bottom tier of Jaime's wedding cake. I love using unusual colour combinations; I think orange and pink work like a dream together. The bouquet on the bottom tier takes the form of a semi-crescent shape.

Peony Wedding Cake

Cake and Decoration

15cm (6") and 25.5cm (10") oval
fruitcakes

Apricot glaze

1.4kg (3lb) white almond paste

Clear alcohol (e.g. white rum, cherry
or orange liqueur)

1kg (2lb) white sugarpaste mixed
with 1kg (2lb) champagne sugarpaste

Fine purple ribbon to trim the cakes

Broad purple ribbon to trim the
boards

Non-toxic glue stick

SK Cocoa Butter

SK Daffodil, Forest Green, Holly/Ivy,
Poinsettia, Rose, Sunflower and
Violet Dust Food Colours

Equipment

20cm (8") and 38cm (15") oval cake
drums

Saucer and mug (or tea light plate
warmer)

Fine paintbrushes

Clear acrylic tilting cake stand (CC)

Non-slip mat

Flowers and Foliage

Peony arrangement
(see pages 104-105)

Preparation

You might prefer to use a polystyrene
dummy cake for the top tier of this cake.
The method described here is for two rich fruitcakes.

1. Brush both cakes with apricot glaze and cover with white almond paste. Allow
to dry, at least overnight. Mix equal amounts of white and champagne
sugarpaste together to make an off-white paste. Moisten the surface of the
almond paste with clear alcohol and cover with sugarpaste. Smooth over the
surface with a pair of sugarpaste smoothers. Cover the cake drums with the
same sugarpaste and trim the edges. Transfer the covered cakes to sit centrally
on top of each board. Allow to dry.

2. Attach a band of fine purple ribbon around the base of each cake. Secure with a
tiny amount of royal icing or a softened sugarpaste/clear alcohol mixture. Glue
a length of broad purple ribbon to the edge of each board using a non-toxic
glue stick.

Side Design

3. The floral design was painted freehand onto the cakes. However, I have
supplied a template on page 141 if you would prefer to trace and scribe it onto
the cakes. Melt some cocoa butter on a saucer over a mug of just boiled water
or on top a tea-light plate warmer. Add each colour in turn to complete the
design: I have used Forest Green and Holly/Ivy for the leaves; Rose and
Poinsettia mixed together for the flower petals and buds; Sunflower mixed
with Daffodil for the stamens; and Violet for the smaller flowers.

Assembly

4. Place the clear acrylic tilting stand on top of the larger cake. Place a piece of
non-slip mat onto the tilt of the stand, and position the smaller cake or
dummy cake on top.

Arrange the flowers as described on pages 104 to 105. Position the
arrangement onto the board of the larger cake. Rearrange the flowers and
foliage to curve around and complement the cake.

This striking red and purple floral wedding cake design features a single red peony combined with freesias, Codiaeum foliage and ivy. The side design has been painted using a mixture of melted cocoa butter and Dust Food Colours.

Materials

18, 20, 24, 26, 28 and 30-gauge white wires

Mid Holly/Ivy coloured, pale Rose coloured and white flower paste

Nile green floristry tape

SK Daffodil, Forest Green, Holly/Ivy, Sunflower and Vine Dust Food Colours

Aubergine, deep magenta, ruby and scarlet craft dusts

White, cream or yellow seed head stamens

Non-toxic craft glue

Half-strength SK Confectioners' Glaze

Equipment

Wire cutters

Tree Peony petal cutters: 731-733 (TT)

Ceramic silk veining tool (HP)

Kitchen paper or cupped former

Small rose petal cutters: 278-280 (TT)

Metal ball tool (CC)

Peony leaf cutters: 723-729 (TT)

SK Great Impressions Peony Leaf Veiner

Chinese Peony

Peonies (*Paeonia*) originate from China and have been in cultivation for a thousand years. I have used peonies frequently in various forms over the years as they have instant impact, and fill big spaces efficiently.

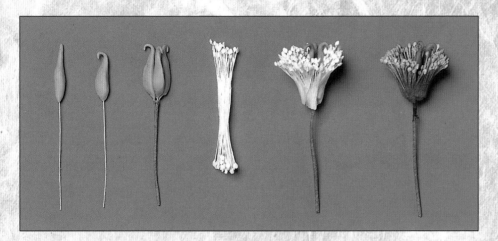

Petals

4. Roll out some pale pink flower paste, leaving a thick ridge for the wire. Cut out a petal using one of the larger peony petal cutters (or the templates on page 142). Insert a moistened, hooked wire into the base of the petal. Vein the petal in a fan formation on both sides using the silk veining tool. Increase the pressure on the edge to create a frilly edge. Hollow out the centre of the petal and allow to dry in a cupped former or a twisted ring of kitchen paper. Repeat to make large and medium sized petals. You will need anything from five to twenty petals, depending upon the variety you are making. I tend to make six medium and nine large petals.

Ovary

1. Cut three short lengths of 26-gauge wire and bend a hook in the end of each. Form a ball of well-kneaded green flower paste into a long teardrop shape and insert a moistened hooked wire into the broad end. Pinch a ridge down the length of the teardrop. Curl the tip over onto the side of the ridge. Repeat to make three sections. While the three sections are still pliable tape them together using half-width Nile green floristry tape. Dust with Vine Dust Food Colour and tinge the tips with a mixture of ruby and aubergine craft dusts. Tape onto an 18-gauge wire. Allow to dry.

Stamens

2. Glue together a group of stamens using a small amount of non-toxic craft glue (or flower paste and egg white mixed together to form a sugar glue, see Important Note on page 133). Squeeze the glue at the centre of the bunch to flatten and secure them together. Leave enough length at either end of the stamens so that they look like individual stamens in the flower. Allow to set. Cut in half and trim to make them a little shorter if necessary. Repeat to make six groups. Glue the stamens around the ovary using either the non-toxic craft glue or sugar glue. Squeeze them tightly to secure them in place.

3. Dust the tips of the stamens with a mixture of Daffodil and Sunflower Dust Food Colours, and colour the length with scarlet craft dust. Curl the stamens out slightly to give a more natural effect.

Colouring and Assembly

5. Dust each petal heavily with a mixture of scarlet and deep magenta craft dusts. You will need to scrub the colour into the paste using a brush to get it to stick. Tinge the edges with some ruby dust. Add a patch of ruby at the base to create depth.

6. Tape the small petals around the stamens, and then the larger ones. Aim to position each petal over a join in the previous layer. Do not try to overlap the petals.

Calyx

7. The calyx has three rounded sepals and two longer, narrow, almost leaf like sepals. Roll out some green flower paste, leaving a thick ridge down the centre. Cut out one of the three sizes of smaller rose petal shapes (or see templates on page 142). Insert a hooked, moistened 30-gauge white wire into the ridge from the pointed end of the sepal. Soften the edge and hollow out the centre using a ball tool. Pinch a slight point in the centre of the rounded edge. Repeat with the other two sizes of rose petal cutter so that you have three rounded sepals.

Buds

10. Roll a ball of white flower paste. Insert a hooked, moistened 18 or 20-gauge wire into the base. Pinch the paste around the wire to secure the two together. Allow to dry.

8. To make the narrow sepals, wrap a piece of green paste around a 30-gauge wire. Thin and form the paste into a narrow teardrop shape. Place the shape on the board and flatten it using the smooth side of a rubber veiner. Pinch the sepal to create a central vein. Repeat to make two long sepals. Dust all of the sepals with Vine and Holly/Ivy Dust Food Colours. Catch the edge with aubergine and ruby craft dusts.

11. Roll out some pink flower paste thinly. Cut out five petals using the smallest of the peony petal cutters. Vein and frill in the same way as for the flower. Moisten each petal and attach them in opposites onto the dried base. Crease the petals as you attach them to create a tight bud shape. Trim off any excess paste if necessary.

9. Tape the three rounded sepals behind the petals on the flower. Space them out and then add the two narrow sepals in-between joins and opposite each other. Bend the long sepals back slightly.

12. Dust the buds to match the flower. Add a calyx as for the flower, except this time the three rounded rose petal sepal shapes are unwired and attached directly onto the bud. Add the two wired sepals as before.

Leaves

13. Roll out some green flower paste, leaving a thick ridge down the centre and cut out a leaf shape. There are several shapes and sizes of peony leaf cutters available; here, I have made one large central leaf with two smaller ones either side. Use the peony leaf cutters (or the templates on page 142). Insert a moistened 28, 26 or 24-gauge wire, depending on the size of the leaf. Soften the edges and vein using the peony leaf veiner. I have used a single leaf veiner, and generally use it to vein the larger tri-lobed leaves on each third. Pinch to reinforce the central vein, and pinch the tip into a neat point.

14. Dust the edges of the leaves with a mixture of aubergine and ruby craft dusts. Use Forest Green to add depth to the base and central areas of the leaves. Over-dust the leaves with Vine and Holly/Ivy Dust Food Colours. Allow to dry. Dip into half-strength confectioners' glaze.

15. Tape the leaves in sets of three. Add the smaller sets of foliage behind each bud and flower. Gradually increase the size of the leaves down the stem. Dust each stem with Holly/Ivy and tinge one side of the stem with aubergine. Rub some non-toxic glue down the stems to set the colour and give them a shine.

Freesia

Materials

22, 24, 26 and 33-gauge white wires
Nile green and white floristry tape
White seed head stamens
Holly/Ivy coloured (optional) and
white flower paste
African violet and plum craft dusts
SK Daffodil, Edelweiss, Forest Green,
Holly/Ivy, Leaf Green, Sunflower and
Vine Dust Food Colours

Equipment

Wire cutters
Small and large CelSticks
Six-petal blossom cutters: 521,
522 (TT) or templates, see page 142
Scalpel
Medium and small metal ball tools
(CC)
Dresden tool (Jem)
Sharp, curved scissors
Plain-edge cutting wheel (PME)
Fine-nosed pliers
Cotton wool

There are around 20 species of freesia and they are all indigenous to South Africa. It is the hybrid forms that most of us are familiar with, often seen as cut and bridal flowers. The method described here is quicker than most and involves a curious wire framework for the buds.

Pistil and Stamens

1. Cut a short length of 33-gauge wire. Tape over with quarter-width white floristry tape, leaving a flap of tape at the end of the wire. Cut the flap into three sections. Twist each section a little to make them finer. On the real flower each third is spilt into two or three, however in this version it is enough to have a pistil spilt into three. Tape onto the end of a 26 or 24-gauge wire using Nile green floristry tape.

2. Cut the tips from both ends of three white seed head stamens. Attach a tiny sausage of white paste onto one end of each stamen. Blend the paste onto the stamen to make the anther finer. Tape the three stamens onto one side of the pistil.

3. Dust the anthers to match the colour of the flower you are making; in this case I used a mixture of African violet and plum craft dusts.

Flower

4. Form a ball of well-kneaded white flower paste into a cone. Pinch out the broad end of the cone to make a hat shape. Place the flat side of the shape down against a non-stick board. Roll and thin out the 'brim' of the hat shape using a CelStick. Cut out the flower shape using a six-

petal blossom cutter, or the templates on page 142. The paste generally sticks in the cutter, allowing you to rub your thumb over the sugar against the cutter to get rid of any rough edges.

5. Place the flower back onto the board. Make a slender 'V' shaped cut using a sharp scalpel in-between each of the petals. Roll each petal with a CelStick to form a slightly pointed tip, then use the same tool to broaden each of the petals.

6. Pick up the flower and open up the throat using the pointed end of a large CelStick. Keep pressing the paste against the tool to thin out the sides of the flower and create more of a characteristic freesia shape.

7. Hollow out the length of each petal using a small ball tool. Add a few central lines to each petal using the fine end of a Dresden tool. Moisten the base of the stamens and pull them through the centre of the flower. Pinch the base of the flower onto the wire to form a finer, more tapered finish to the flower. Add some fine veining on the sides of the flower using either a scalpel or plain edge-cutting wheel.

8. Rearrange the position of the petals a little so that there are three inner and three outer alternate petals. Make some flowers more open than others. You might also prefer to make some smaller flowers using the smallest cutter.

Calyx

9. You can either make two snips into the base of the flower to create a calyx, or add a calyx made from green flower paste. I usually use the former method.

Wire Frame and Buds

10. Tape over the length of a 24-gauge wire with quarter or half-width Nile green floristry tape. Bend a tight hook in the end of the wire using fine-nosed pliers. Work along the stem slightly using a nipping, pinching movement with the pliers to curve the stem in-between each of the hooks for each bud. Buckle and twist another loop and continue the buckling and twisting to make about five to seven sections. These twisted loops form the framework on which to add the paste buds. Make sure that the loops graduate a little in size and that they are not too open.

11. Next, mould a paste bud onto each loop. Squeeze the paste at the base of each bud to form a finer neck. Create a calyx on each bud as described for the flower. Bend the buds so that they alternate in position from left to right or right to left.

Colouring and Assembly

12. Dust the base and middle section with a little Daffodil, Sunflower and Edelweiss Dust Food Colours mixed together. Add a dash or streak of yellow inside the throat of the flower. Over-dust the base of the flower with some Vine. Colour the calyx darker with a mixture of Leaf Green, Holly/Ivy and Forest Green.

13. It is difficult to colour the flower petals as the colour tends to blend with the yellow inside the throat, resulting in a dirty finish. It is best to plug the centre with a piece of clean, rolled up cotton wool. Dust the edges with your chosen flower colour – in this instance I have used a mixture of plum and African violet craft dusts.

Dust the buds as for the flowers. Increase the green colouring on the smaller buds, gradually fading it out to allow the true flower colour to dominate.

14. Bend the stem a little from the last bud and then start to add the flowers.

Codiaeum Foliage

These are commonly known as Crotons,
however the Croton family is separate from the
Codiaeum family, and is of more medicinal than decorative value. These leaves
are highly decorative and useful for their variation in colour.

Materials

Pale cream flower paste

22 or 24-gauge white wires

SK Daffodil, Forest Green, Holly/Ivy,
Leaf Green, Rose, Sunflower and
Vine Dust Food Colours

Aubergine and coral craft dusts

SK Glaze Cleaner (Isopropyl Alcohol)

Half or three quarter-strength SK
Confectioners' Glaze

Equipment

Plain-edge cutting wheel (PME)

Leaf templates (see page 143)

SK Great Impressions Poinsettia
Veiner (very large or extra large), or
similar

Leaves

1. Roll out the paste so that it is quite fleshy, leaving a central ridge for the wire. Cut out a leaf shape freehand using the plain-edge cutting wheel. The leaves can vary from a fairly plain edge to more complicated semi and full tri-sectioned foliage (see templates on page 143). Insert a moistened 22 or 24-gauge wire into the thick ridge. Soften the edge and then vein in a large poinsettia veiner or similar. Pinch the leaf from the base to the tip to emphasize the central vein. Allow to firm up a little before colouring.

Colouring

2. Paint the central and side veins and the edge of the leaf with a mixture of Rose Dust Food Colour and isopropyl alcohol. Allow to dry. Next, mix up a green paint using Holly/Ivy, Forest Green and Leaf Green mixed with isopropyl alcohol. Paint the sections in-between each of the finer red veins. Fade the amount of colour as you get to the tip of the leaf. Allow to dry.

3. Dust over the top of the painted veining with Sunflower, Rose, Holly/Ivy and Vine Dust Food Colours until you have achieved the desired effect. It is best to have a real leaf or good picture to copy when you colour the foliage. Dip into half or three quarter-strength confectioners' glaze. Allow to dry.

Peony Arrangement

Flowers and Foliage

1 red peony and bud

5 sets of peony foliage

8 Codiaeum leaves

5 stems of freesia

7 trailing stems of ivy

(see pages 74-75)

Equipment

18-gauge wire

Nile green floristry tape

Wire cutters

Small glass tea light holder

Florists' Staysoft

Fine-nosed pliers

Preparation

1. First of all you will need to strengthen some of the flower and foliage stems by taping an additional 18-gauge wire onto each stem. Trim the stems using wire cutters as you work through the arrangement.

2. Fill the glass tea light holder with some florists' Staysoft. Bend a hook in the end of the peony flower and bud stems using a pair of fine-nosed pliers. Insert the flower stem into the Staysoft. This flower will form the focal point of the arrangement. Next, add the peony bud stem so that it stands high above the flower. Add the peony foliage to help frame the flower. Continue to frame the peony flower and fill in the large area around it using the Codiaeum leaves.

3. Arrange the five stems of freesia into the design to create extra height and fill in some gaps in the arrangement.

Finally, add several trailing stems of ivy to complete the design. Stand back from the arrangement and make any necessary adjustments.

The strong red, yellow and green markings of the Codiaeum foliage help to hold this bold colour scheme of purple and red together. I often find arrangements with fewer flowers combined with lots of foliage forms a more pleasing effect.

Fidelity

Ivy is often used as a symbol of fidelity, making it the perfect addition to the richly coloured roses and dahlia on this heart-shaped wedding cake. This single-tiered design is ideal for a small, intimate reception.

Cake and Decoration

17.5cm (7") heart shaped fruitcake

Apricot glaze

500g (1lb) white almond paste

Clear alcohol (e.g. white rum, cherry or orange liqueur)

500g (1lb) pale pink sugarpaste

Broad pink organza-type ribbon to trim the cake

Equipment

17.5cm (7") heart shaped board

Non-slip mat

Clear acrylic tilting cake stand (CC)

Food-grade posy pick

Flowers and Foliage

2 dahlia flowers, plus foliage

2 dahlia buds

1 rosebud (see page 82)

1 half rose (see page 82)

3 carnations (see pages 12-14)

7 Honesty seed heads

7 Coleus leaves

8 stems of trailing ivy
(see pages 74-75)

Preparation

1. Position the cake on top of a board of the same size and shape and brush with apricot glaze. Cover both the cake and the edge of the board with almond paste. Allow the almond paste to dry before moistening the surface with clear alcohol. Cover the cake and board as a whole with pink sugarpaste. Trim the edge and smooth over the surface with sugarpaste smoothers. Allow to dry.

Attach a band of pink organza-style ribbon around the base of the cake using a small amount of sugarpaste softened with clear alcohol.

Assembly

2. Place a non-slip mat onto the tilt of the clear acrylic stand and position the cake on top. Arrange a few trailing stems of ivy around the base of the tilting stand. Wire together the dahlia and rose spray (see pages 114-115), insert a food-grade plastic posy pick into the top of the cake and position the handle of the spray into it. Rearrange the ivy attractively over the surface of the cake.

Dahlia

Dahlias were one of the favourite plants of the Aztecs. The genus comprises of around twenty species found in Mexico and Central America. The tuber of the plant had at one stage been introduced into Europe as a supplement for the potato, however they proved to be unpalatable. The colour range and shape of many of the cultivated forms is vast.

Materials

22, 24, 26, 28 and 30-gauge white wires

Cream and mid-Holly/Ivy coloured flower paste

Nile green floristry tape

SK Daffodil, Forest Green, Holly/Ivy, Sunflower and Vine Dust Food Colours

SK Glaze Cleaner (Isopropyl Alcohol)

Aubergine and plum craft dusts

Half-strength SK Confectioners' Glaze

Equipment

Single petal daisy cutters: 612-614 (TT)

Ruscus cutters: 2, 5, 8, 11, 325 (TT) or Gaura leaf cutter set: 870-872 (TT) (optional, for larger flowers)

Fine-nosed pliers

Sharp scalpel

Plain-edge cutting wheel (PME)

Metal ball tool (CC)

Silk veining tool (HP)

Dresden Tool (Jem) (optional)

Eight-petal daisy cutters

SK Great Impressions Dahlia Leaf Veiners

Flower Centre and Opening Buds

1. Decide on the size and shape of flower you want to make. The flowers pictured were made using the single petal daisy cutter set. They are very narrow and need to be altered slightly using fine-nosed pliers to create a broader petal shape. If you decide to make larger flowers, alternative cutters are listed opposite.

2. Bend a small, open hook in the end of a 22-gauge white wire. Form a small cone of cream flower paste. Moisten the wire and insert the hook into the broad end of the cone. Work the base of the cone onto the wire to secure it in place. Divide the cone into eight sections using either a sharp scalpel or a cutting wheel. Allow to dry.

3. Roll out some cream flower paste and cut out eight petals using the smallest cutter you intend to use. Soften the edges with a ball tool. Broaden and vein each petal slightly using the silk veining tool. Draw down a few stronger veins using the Dresden tool or cutting wheel.

4. The petals can be curled in or out on a dahlia, depending on the variety. Curl and pinch each of the petals together. Moisten the cone and attach all eight petals. Repeat the process a few times, increasing the size of cutter accordingly to make the required size of opening bud or the base from which you will add the following wired petals. Aim to position each petal in-between the petals of the previous layer.

Wired Petals

5. Roll out some more cream coloured flower paste, this time leaving a thick ridge for a fine wire. Cut out a petal shape using a slightly larger petal cutter than the one used for the outer layer of the flower centre. Insert a 30 or 28-gauge wire, depending on the size of petal. Pinch the base of the petal onto the wire to elongate it slightly. Soften the edges with a ball tool. Broaden and vein the petal gently using the silk veining tool. Draw a few extra, stronger veins onto the petal. Pinch the petal to curl it in or out to match the petals of the flower centre.

Repeat to make eight petals for each layer. It is a good idea to make extra sizes of wired petals so that a variation of flower size can be created. Allow to dry slightly.

6. Tape the wired petals onto the flower centre using half-width Nile green floristry tape. Position each petal in-between the petals on the previous layer.

Colouring

7. Dust the flower as required. The flowers pictured here are dusted using a light mixture of Sunflower, Daffodil and Edelweiss at the base of each petal, and then painted with a mixture of isopropyl alcohol with plum and aubergine craft dusts. Finally, dust over the paintwork with the same colour to hide any streaks on the petals.

Calyx

8. Roll out some green flower paste and cut out two eight-petal daisy shapes – the size will depend on the size of the flower or bud you have made. Soften each sepal and draw down a central vein on each one. Attach both calyces to the back of the flower; one calyx should be up against the petals and the other should curl back. Pinch the tips slightly.

Dust with a mixture of Vine and Holly/Ivy Dust Food Colours.

Leaves

9. Roll out some green flower paste, leaving a thick ridge down the centre. Press the flat side of one of the dahlia leaf veiners onto the paste to leave a leaf shaped outline. Cut out the leaf using a sharp scalpel or plain-edge cutting wheel.

10. Insert a moistened 28, 26 or 24-gauge wire into the leaf. Soften the edges and vein using the two sides of the dahlia leaf veiner. Pinch the central vein to accentuate it. Repeat to make leaves in sets of three and five.

11. The colouring of the foliage varies. I have used aubergine on the edges to match the dark flowers and then dusted in layers with Forest Green, Holly/Ivy and a touch of Vine. The colouring should be heavier on the front of the leaf than the back.

Dip into half-strength confectioners' glaze. Tape the leaves together in groups.

111

Honesty Seed Heads

I have chosen to make Honesty seed heads in their green, almost ripened stage. Honesty (*Lunaria annua*) is an annual plant. It has pretty, violet, four-petalled flowers that die off to leave these curious seed heads. When fully ripened, they peel to reveal a silvery, papery seed head that is often used in dried flower arrangements.

Materials

33-gauge white wires

White floristry tape

Black-grey and pale Holly/Ivy coloured flower paste

SK Forest Green, Holly/Ivy, Leaf Green and Vine Dust Food Colours

Aubergine craft dust

SK Glaze Cleaner (Isopropyl Alcohol)

Equipment

Fine-nosed pliers

Bougainvillea cutters (Jem)

Ceramic silk veining tool (HP)

Sharp fine scissors

Stencil brush

Seed Heads

1. The seed head is formed on a wire frame. Bend a length of 33-gauge wire in half, then twist a small point at the bend using fine-nosed pliers. Curve out both halves of the wire to form the basic oval shape of the seed head. Twist the wires together at the base of the oval to complete the shape. Tape over the stem with white floristry tape. Tie a knot in the wire stem.

2. Roll and flatten some small balls of black-grey flower paste to form the seeds. Roll out some pale green paste very thinly. Cut out two bougainvillea bract shapes. Soften the edges. Make a few indents using the round end of a ceramic silk veining tool.

   Moisten the wire frame and attach it to one of the shapes. Position a few seeds onto the paste, and then sandwich the other shape on top. Press them together firmly or gently, depending upon the ripeness of the seed head. Trim around the edges with fine, sharp scissors to follow the line of the wire framework.

3. Dust with Leaf Green and Vine Dust Food Colours. Add a touch of depth with a light dusting of Holly/Ivy and Forest Green. Dust or paint the edge with aubergine craft dust. Load a stencil brush with diluted colour and flick this over the seed heads in places.

Coleus

Materials

Pale Rose coloured flower paste

24 and 26-gauge wires

Aubergine, deep magenta and sap green craft dusts

SK Forest Green and Holly/Ivy Dust Food Colours

SK Glaze Cleaner (Isopropyl Alcohol)

Quarter-strength SK Confectioners' Glaze (optional)

Equipment

Coleus leaf templates (see page 143)

Sharp scalpel or plain-edge cutting wheel (PME)

Medium metal ball tool (CC)

Coleus leaf or SK Great Impressions Ornamental Nettle Veiners

Ceramic silk veining tool (HP)

There are several species and many more cultivars of Coleus. Although the plants are often grown as houseplants, these ornamental, nettle-like plants are originally from Java. I have chosen one of the larger leaved varieties.

Leaves

1. Colour some flower paste pale pink using SK Rose Paste Food Colour. If you are unsure of the exact finished colour you want the leaf to be, it is wise to use a cream coloured paste instead. Roll out some paste, leaving a suitably thick ridge for the wire.

   Place a leaf template on top of the paste and cut around it using either a sharp scalpel or plain-edge cutting wheel. Don't worry if you are not very accurate as these leaves can vary considerably in shape.

2. Insert a moistened 24 or 26-gauge wire, depending upon the exact size of the leaf. Place the leaf on a pad and soften the edges using a medium metal ball tool, working half on the paste and half on the pad with a rolling action.

3. Place the leaf into a suitable veiner and press the two sides firmly together. Remove the leaf from the veiner and pinch down the length from the back of the leaf at the base to the tip to accentuate the central vein.

   Frill each section of the leaf edge using a ceramic silk veining tool. Allow to dry fairly flat before colouring.

Colouring

4. Dust from the centre of the leaf on the back and the front using deep magenta craft dust. Next, mix together some Forest Green, sap green and Holly/Ivy and dust inwards from the edge of the leaf. Dilute some of the colour with isopropyl alcohol to make it more intense and paint extra markings on the edge of the leaf. The paint should dry quite quickly. Over-dust the edges with aubergine.

   Pass the leaves over steam to set the colour, or dip into quarter-strength confectioners' glaze.

113

Dahlia and Rose Spray

Dark aubergine coloured roses and dahlias form the main interest in this unusual spray. Magenta streaked carnations and Coleus foliage help to lighten the spray without detracting from the stronger focal flowers.

Flowers and Foliage

2 dahlia buds

2 dahlia flowers, plus foliage

1 rosebud (see page 82)

1 half rose (see page 82)

7 Coleus leaves

7 Honesty seed heads

3 carnations (see pages 12-14)

8 stems of trailing ivy
(see pages 74-75)

Equipment

20-gauge floristry wires

Nile green floristry tape

Wire cutters

Fine-nosed pliers

Preparation

1. Start by taping the two dahlia buds with some foliage using half-width Nile green floristry tape. If required, strengthen the wires with 20-gauge wires. Tape in the two larger dahlias next, surrounded by more dahlia foliage. Fill in any gaps in the spray with the rosebud and half rose. Next, tape in a circle of Coleus to surround the flowers and dahlia foliage. Trim away any excess wires as you work.

2. Tape together two sets of green Honesty seed heads. Add these opposite each other on either side of the spray. Add a line of carnations in the opposite direction to the Honesty seed heads. You will need to use fine-nosed pliers to insert the stems into the spray and avoid damaging the flowers. Finally, add trails of ivy to complete the spray.

NOTE: The roses were made with cream coloured flower paste and then dusted, painted and dusted again in layers with plum and aubergine craft dust and isopropyl alcohol. The carnations were made with pale Vine coloured paste and the edges painted with plum craft dust mixed with isopropyl alcohol. I also used a stencil brush loaded with the diluted bright pink colour to fleck spots onto each flower.

Tulipa

A tied bunch of parrot tulips and mistletoe have been tangled together with a wired string of coloured glass beads, forming a very simple and yet pretty centrepiece.

Cake and Decoration

25.5cm (10") teardrop shaped rich fruitcake

Apricot glaze

1kg (2lb) white almond paste

Clear alcohol (e.g. white rum, cherry or orange liqueur)

1kg (2lb) white sugarpaste

Broad magenta ribbon

Wired string of coloured beads

Nile green floristry tape

18-gauge wire

Equipment

25.5cm (10") teardrop shaped board

Fine food-grade posy pick (CC)

Pliers

Flowers and Foliage

2 parrot tulip buds

3 parrot tulips

7 tulip leaves

3 sprigs of mistletoe (see page 131)

Preparation

1. Position the cake on a board of the same shape and size. Brush the surface with apricot glaze and cover the whole thing with white almond paste. Allow to dry overnight. Moisten the surface with clear alcohol and cover with white sugarpaste. Smooth over the surface using sugarpaste smoothers, and carefully trim the edge to form a neat finish. Allow to dry.

2. Attach a broad band of magenta coloured ribbon around the base of the cake using a small amount of sugarpaste softened with clear alcohol.

Floral Spray

3. Start the tied bunch of flowers with a couple of parrot tulip buds and a couple of sprigs of mistletoe. Start to tangle and tie in the wired string of glass beads. Gradually add the full-blown parrot tulips to create the main body of the tied bunch. Add extra sprigs of mistletoe and frame the spray with the parrot tulip leaves.

4. Insert a fine posy pick into the cake. Fill the pick with a small amount of white almond paste. Cut a couple of short lengths of 18-gauge wire. Bend them over using a pair of pliers (these 'pins' are used to hold the spray in position on the cake). Place the handle of the spray over the filled pick, and then carefully place the 'pins' over a few of the wire stems, inserting their ends into the almond paste in the posy pick.

Arrange the excess length of wired beads over and around the shape of the cake. Tuck the end of the wire back into the spray to complete the display.

Parrot Tulip

It is hardly surprising that the tulip has long been a favourite subject for artists and craftsmen alike. Four hundred years of growers' obsession and skill have produced a huge variation of blooms. Parrot tulips can occur in single, semi and double forms in a huge range and variation of colours.

Materials

Pale Holly/Ivy coloured and white flower paste

18, 22, 24, 26 and 33-gauge white wires

Nile green floristry tape

SK Edelweiss, Daffodil, Forest Green, Holly/Ivy, Leaf Green and Vine Dust Food Colours

African violet, aubergine and plum craft dusts

SK Glaze Cleaner (Ispopropyl Alcohol)

Quarter-strength SK Confectioners' Glaze (optional)

Equipment

Angled tweezers

Plain edge cutting wheel (PME)

Scalpel (optional)

Wire cutters

Parrot tulip cutter (CC)

Dresden tool (PME)

Medium metal ball tool (CC)

Kitchen paper

Large scissors

SK Great Impressions Tulip Leaf Veiner

Pistil

1. Take a small ball of white or pale green flower paste and form it into a sausage shape. Insert a moistened 22-gauge wire. Work the paste onto the wire to secure it in place, removing the excess paste as you go. The length of the pistil will depend on the size of petals you are planning to make – I usually make it no longer than an inch in length. Flatten the tip a little, and then pinch the shape into three sections using a pair of angled tweezers (preferably without 'teeth' on them). Pull out the sections with your finger and thumb to both define them and create a flatter shape on the top. Add a few lines using a scalpel blade or a plain-edge cutting wheel. If you are making double parrot tulips then this centre can be doubled (and should look more wrinkly than the single form).

Stamens

2. Cut a short length of 33-gauge wire. The number of stamens can vary between single, semi and double flowers. Generally a single flower has only six stamens, whilst the others have a few and often many more, Take a small ball of white paste and insert a short wire into it. Blend and work the paste down onto the wire to form the filament. Trim off any excess paste. Flatten the shape onto the wire and taper the tip into a point. Add an extra teardrop piece of paste to form the anther. Flatten it and draw a line down each side using the plain-edge cutting wheel.

3. Dust the pistil with a light mixture of Edelweiss and Vine Dust Food Colours. Dust the filaments of the stamens using the same mixture. The anthers

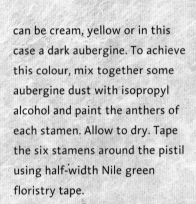

can be cream, yellow or in this case a dark aubergine. To achieve this colour, mix together some aubergine dust with isopropyl alcohol and paint the anthers of each stamen. Allow to dry. Tape the six stamens around the pistil using half-width Nile green floristry tape.

Petals

4. The number of petals can vary from six upwards, depending upon the variety. I usually use six petals for each flower. Roll out some white flower paste, leaving a thick ridge down the centre for the wire. Cut out a petal shape using the parrot tulip petal cutter. Insert a moistened 26-gauge wire into about a third of the length of the ridge. Place the petal onto a non-stick board and, using the broad end of a Dresden tool, create some veining by pulling the paste out in a 'V' shape from the base of the petal. Next, increase the pressure on the edge of the petal to create

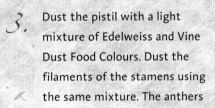

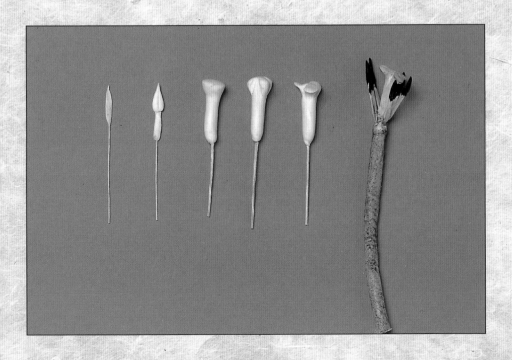

a slightly frilled effect. Cut into the edges of the petal in-between each scallop using the fine end of the veining tool. Add extra smaller cuts around the whole of the shape.

5. Place the petal onto a pad and draw two lines onto the petal using the plain-edge cutting wheel. Turn the petal over and add a single vein down the centre of the petal.

Next, hollow out each section of the inside part of the petal using the small end of a medium metal ball tool. Make a former from a twisted piece of kitchen paper tied into a ring shape. Pinch the petal from the base through to the tip and allow to firm up a little on the former before colouring. Repeat to make the required number of petals.

Colouring and Assembly

6. Dust the edges of each petal with a mixture of plum, African violet and Edelweiss. Use a light mixture of Vine and Edelweiss to dust the inside at outer surface from the base to about halfway up the petal. Mix some Holly/Ivy, Leaf Green and Vine together with a touch of Edelweiss and mix with some isopropyl alcohol. Paint some green streaks onto the back of each petal. Increase the depth of the colour a little as you work to create a more interesting design.

7. Tape three petals around the base of the stamens. Add an extra 18-gauge wire if you are planning to use long stemmed tulips. Add the remaining three petals in-between the first three to complete the flower. If you have made more petals, continue to add them over the gaps in each previous layer. It is wise to colour and assemble the flower before the paste has dried so that you can bend and re-shape them to form a more realistic shape. Thicken the stem using full-width Nile green floristry tape. You might prefer to shred a length of kitchen paper to wrap around and tape over the stem. Polish the stem using the sides of a large pair of scissors.

Buds

8. Bend a hook in the end of an 18-gauge wire. Roll a ball of well-kneaded flower paste and form it into a pointed tulip bud shape. Insert the moistened wire into the base. Divide the bud into three sections using either the cutting wheel or a sharp knife. Create a couple of central veins on each section using the small end of the cutting wheel.

9. Roll out some white paste and cut out three petals using the parrot tulip cutter. Re-cut into each petal using the same cutter to make each petal smaller and more suitable to fit the bud. Vein and work each petal as described for the flower. Curl the edges of each

petal in slightly as you moisten and add them over joins in the marked petals on the bud. Thicken the stem as for the flowers. Colour as described for the wired flower petals, adding more green colour on the small buds.

Leaves

10. Roll out some pale green flower paste, leaving a thick ridge down the centre. Cut out a wide, long leaf freehand. Insert a 26, 24, or 22-gauge white wire into the thick ridge. Soften the edges and then vein using the tulip leaf veiner. Pinch the leaf to accentuate the central vein. Dust lightly in layers with Forest Green, Holly/Ivy and Edelweiss Dust Food Colours. Pass over steam or dip into a quarter-strength confectioners' glaze.

Blushing Bride

Cake and Decoration

17.5cm (7") heart shaped rich fruitcake

Apricot glaze

500g (1lb) white almond paste

Clear alcohol (e.g. white rum, cherry or orange liqueur)

750g (1lb 10oz) champagne sugarpaste

Narrow green ribbon to trim the cake

Small amount of cream flower paste

Broad pale green decorative ribbon to trim the board edge

Non-toxic glue stick

Nile green floristry tape

Copper wire

Small amount of royal icing (optional)

SK Leaf Green, Rose and Vine Dust Food Colours

SK White Satin Bridal Satin Lustre Dust Colour

Equipment

25.5cm (10") heart shaped drum

2 fine food-grade posy picks (CC)

Small star cutter

Single petal daisy cutter

Flowers and Foliage

3 Blushing Bride protea flowers

6 Blushing Bride protea buds

Several sets of protea leaves

Blushing Bride protea flowers with their fern-like foliage have been used to create this delicate single tier cake suitable for a small wedding reception. Twisted copper wire has been added to the sprays of flowers to add a little interest to this simple cake design.

Preparation

1. Brush the cake with apricot glaze and cover with white almond paste. Allow to dry overnight. Moisten the surface with clear alcohol and cover with champagne sugarpaste. Use a pair of sugarpaste smoothers to create a smooth finish. Cover the cake board with sugarpaste and position the cake offset on top of it. Use a smoother to work the paste around the base of the cake down against the paste on the board to form a neat join.

2. Attach a band of green ribbon around the base of the cake using a small amount of royal icing or a softened sugarpaste/clear alcohol mixture. Attach a band of pale green ribbon to the board edge using a non-toxic glue stick.

3. Wire together two sprays of Blushing Bride flowers, buds and foliage using half-width Nile green floristry tape. Add twisted lengths of copper wire to both sprays. Insert two posy picks into the cake and then insert the handle of each spray into them as pictured.

Side Design

4. Mix together a small amount of cream flower paste with some champagne sugarpaste. Roll out the paste thinly and cut out some star and petal shapes. Dust the petals with a soft mixture of Leaf Green and Vine Dust Food Colours and White Satin Lustre Dust and dust the stars with a touch of Rose and White Satin Dusts. Moisten the back of each shape and carefully attach them onto the side of the cake. I have used five-petal shapes together with a star at the centre to form a naïve abstract floral design. A few star shapes have also been used together in other areas on the cake surface.

Blushing Bride Protea

Materials

Fine white lace makers' thread
(120-gauge)
22, 24, 26, 30 and 33-gauge white
wires
White and pale green floristry tape
SK Edelweiss, Forest Green, Holly/Ivy
and Vine Dust Food Colours
Coral and plum craft dusts
White flower paste

Equipment

Emery board
Hi-tack, non-toxic craft glue
Blushing Bride Protea cutters (CCUT)
or squashed Christmas rose cutters:
282-284 (TT)
Medium ball tool (CC)
SK Great Impressions Stargazer B
Petal Veiner

Serruria is an evergreen shrub which is native to South Africa. It belongs to the *proteaceae* family and the flowers are often known as Blushing Bride. There are several varieties and hybrid forms; one variety is called Sugar and Spice! At first glance there appears to be a mass of stamens at the centre of each flower – these fluffy parts are actually the true flowers. The papery bracts can be white, cream, pink or coral/red tinged.

Flower Centre

I have used a touch of artistic licence with my flower centre, creating a bushy, fluffy centre more suited to a mature flower. The real thing is a little more detailed than my version.

1. Wrap some white thread around two slightly parted fingers about 50-60 times. Remove the loop from your fingers and twist into a figure of eight, and then bend in half to form a smaller loop. Insert a 26-gauge wire through the centre of the thread and bend both ends of the wire together. Tape tightly over the base of the thread and down the wire with white floristry tape.

2. Cut open the thread and trim back to a 2.5cm (1") length. Rub the tips of the thread on an emery board to fray the ends. Next, apply a very light coating of non-toxic craft glue to hold this group of fluff together (fresh egg white may also be used, see Important Note on page 133). Allow to dry. Cut some extra lengths of thread, fluff up the tips and glue around the main centre. Allow to dry. Seed head stamens can also be added to the centre to create a little more interest if required.

3. Dust with a light mixture of Vine and Edelweiss Dust Food Colours. Mix together coral, plum and Edelweiss dusts and add tinges or streaks to the stamens.

Bracts

4. (As explained above these are bracts not petals.) Roll out some white flower paste thinly, leaving a slight ridge down the centre. Cut out a bract shape using one of the four sizes of Blushing Bride protea cutters or squash a set of Christmas rose cutters to make a narrower petal shape.

5. Insert a moistened 33-gauge wire into the thick ridge, holding the bract firmly to avoid the wire piercing through the paste. Soften the edge using a medium ball tool, working half on the edge of the bract and half on your hand/pad. Vein, using the Stargazer B petal veiner. Pinch the petal firmly from the base through to the tip. Repeat to make numerous bracts using all four sizes of cutters. The flower heads vary in how they are grouped. I usually make ten bracts of each size; whatever is left over I use on one of the bracts or the next flower.

6. Tape the bracts around the centre whilst they are still pliable using white or very pale green floristry tape, allowing time to re-shape them as they are attached. Start with a few of the smaller bracts and then add a ring of the largest bracts. Continue to add more bracts down the stem, gradually reducing them in size as you go.

7. Give each bract a light dusting of Vine and Edelweiss dusts mixed together. The bracts can be completely pale and green tinged, or have pink, red or coral shading, and often have a stronger line of colour on the back of each bract.

Buds

8. Bend a hook in the end of a 24-gauge wire, moisten the end and insert into the rounded base of a pointed cone shape of white paste. Mark into three sections. Allow to dry a little.

9. Tape some medium sized bracts around the bud. It helps if the bracts are still pliable, so that you can squeeze them tightly around the bud to begin with. As for the flower, continue to add the bracts in decreasing sizes. Dust in the same way as for the flower and steam both the flowers and buds.

Foliage

10. Tape over a short length of 33 or 30-gauge white wire using quarter-width pale green floristry tape. Create some side sections of twisted tape and add onto the main middle section. Add the extra pieces in pairs.

Dust with a light mixture of Forest Green, Edelweiss and Holly/Ivy Dust Food Colours. Tape a few sets of leaves onto each stem. I have made a few larger groups of foliage to use in the main spray.

Tillandsia Moss

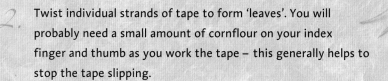

Tillandsia usenoides is one of about four hundred Tillandsia species. It is unusual in that it lacks the usual family trait of water-storing rosette styled foliage. Instead the foliage is covered with water absorbent scales. The plant, which hangs in festoons from trees and telegraph wires in subtropical and tropical America, has tiny blue or pale green flowers and is often used as nesting material by birds. The plant can be dried and dyed various bright colours for use in the floristry trade. It makes a great trailing addition to bouquets and arrangements.

Preparation

1. Shred several lengths of full-width floristry tape through a tape shredder (you will find this wonderful piece of equipment at most good cake decorating shops). There are three razorblades fitted into this gadget to shred fine lengths of thread and you will need to change the razorblades regularly as they become blunt quite quickly. Be extremely careful not to put your fingers anywhere near the blades! It is best to feed the tape through the machine using tweezers. The tape should be cut into four lengths.

2. Twist individual strands of tape to form 'leaves'. You will probably need a small amount of cornflour on your index finger and thumb as you work the tape – this generally helps to stop the tape slipping.

3. As you make each 'leaf', tape it onto the end of a 33-gauge white wire using a little more quarter-width floristry tape. Continue to add the leaves to create the length of trailing stem required. Add an extra 30 or 28-gauge wire if you feel the stem needs a little more support. Some of the leaves may be taped into pairs before they are added onto the main stem.

Colouring

4. To create the natural green-grey colour of the plant, mix together Forest Green, Holly/Ivy, Blackberry and Edelweiss Dust Food Colours. Dust liberally onto the leaves and stem. The new growth of the plant can be slightly greener in colour.

If required, you can spray the finished plant with artists' matt spray varnish.

Materials

White or pale green floristry tape
Cornflour (cornstarch)
28, 30 and 33-gauge white wires
SK Blackberry, Edelweiss, Forest Green and Holly/Ivy Dust Food Colours
Artists' matt spray varnish (optional)

Equipment

Floristry tape shredder (Jem)
Tweezers
Dresden tool (Jem)

Christmas Kisses

Cake and Decoration

15cm (6") round polystyrene dummy cake

23cm (9") and 30.5cm (12") round rich fruitcakes

Apricot glaze

3kg (6$^1/_2$ lb) white almond paste

Clear alcohol (e.g. white rum, cherry or orange liqueur)

5kg (11lb) white sugarpaste

Decorative pale green ribbon to trim the cakes and the board

SK Cocoa Butter

SK Forest Green, Holly/Ivy, Leaf Green and Vine Dust Food Colours

SK White Satin Bridal Satin Lustre Dust

Nile green floristry tape

Equipment

23cm (9") thin round cake board

40cm (16") round cake drum

Non-toxic glue stick

Cup and saucer

Fine paintbrush

Scalpel

Silver circle candleholder (or similar)

4 fine food-grade posy picks (CC)

Flowers and Foliage

Several stems of mistletoe foliage and berries

Silver paper-covered wire

It is often a mistake to overcrowd a cake design with too many different types of flowers and foliage. Simple, light airy sprays of mistletoe berries and foliage have been used to create an instant winter's chill to this elegant three-tier wedding cake.

Preparation

1. I have used a polystyrene dummy cake covered in sugarpaste for the top tier of this design, making it lighter in weight, and also allowing me to insert stems of wired mistletoe into the underside. You might prefer to use real cakes for the whole display, in which case you must ensure that wires are not inserted directly into the cake. If you are using a real cake for the top tier, place it on a thin cake board of the same size, brush it with apricot glaze and cover with white almond paste.

2. Place the middle tier onto a board of the same size and place the bottom tier on a spare board. Brush both cakes with apricot glaze and cover with almond paste. Leave to dry overnight.

3. Brush the surface of the almond paste with clear alcohol and cover with white sugarpaste. If you are using a polystyrene dummy for the top tier, moisten it with clear alcohol and cover only with a layer of white sugarpaste. Use a pair of sugarpaste smoothers to achieve a smooth, polished finish. Allow the three cakes to firm overnight.

4. Lightly moisten the large round cake drum with clear alcohol and cover with sugarpaste. Position the large coated cake on top and use a smoother to create a neat join between the base of the cake and the board. Next, position the middle tier (cake board included) on top of the base tier and once again neaten the join between the two cakes. Allow the three cakes and drum to dry overnight.

5. Attach a band of decorative pale green ribbon around the base of each cake using either royal icing or a small amount of sugarpaste softened with clear alcohol. Attach the ribbon around the board with a non-toxic glue stick.

Side Design

6. The mistletoe design has been painted freehand directly onto the cake. However, you might prefer to trace and then scribe the design onto the cake using the template (see page 143). To make the 'paint', grate a small amount of cocoa butter onto a saucer or palette. Next, melt it over a cup filled with just-boiled water or over a tea light plate warmer. Use the Vine, Holly/Ivy, Leaf Green and Forest Green Dust Food Colours mixed with the melted cocoa butter in turn to paint the stems and leaves onto the cake. Use the lightest green first, gradually adding shadow and detail using the darker greens. Once the leaves are dry, use a sharp scalpel to etch and peel away some highlighted veining from the leaves. Paint the berries using a mixture of the cocoa butter and White Satin Lustre Dust, and then add the detail using a little light green.

Assembly

7. Position the silver candleholder on top of the middle tier. Carefully place the smallest cake on top of it (the candleholder I used has a sharp spike in the middle that helped to hold the polystyrene in place). Insert a few stems of mistletoe into the underside of the dummy cake so that they hang and trail down over the candleholder. If using a real cake, tape the wires to the underside of the board on which it is placed and choose a candleholder with no spike.

8. Tape together four very airy sprays of mistletoe, making the spray for the top tier much larger than the other three. If desired, add some curly lengths of wire covered with silver paper to soften the edges of the sprays and also emulate the spiral design of the candleholder. The top spray can be inserted directly into the polystyrene dummy; you will need to use a posy pick if you are using a real cake. Insert fine posy picks into the middle and bottom tiers, and then insert and position each spray to complete the design.

The Druids used mistletoe in their sacred rituals. Pliny the Elder wrote 1,900 years ago that they would cut down mistletoe with a golden sickle, catching it on a white robe, to stop it falling to the ground where the magic powers of the plant would be drained away. The custom of kissing under hanging mistletoe is a very quirky British tradition. It might have arisen from the Scandinavian belief that the plant was sacred, so when enemies met beneath it in the forest they laid down their arms and maintained a truce all day.

Mistletoe is a semi-parasite, sinking its roots into the host tree (usually apple, hawthorn, poplar, lime and willow).

Materials

Pale Holly/Ivy and white flower paste
26, 28, 30 and 33-gauge white wires
SK White Satin Bridal Satin Lustre Dust
SK Edelweiss, Forest Green, Holly/Ivy, Leaf Green and Vine Dust Food Colours
SK Blackberry Liquid Food Colour or Food Colour Pen
Quarter or half-strength SK Confectioners' Glaze
Nile green floristry tape

Equipment

Tea light or cigarette lighter
Vanilla orchid petal cutters:
827-829 (TT)
Plain-edge cutting wheel (PME)
Metal ball tool (CC)
SK Great Impressions Stargazer B Petal Veiner

Mistletoe

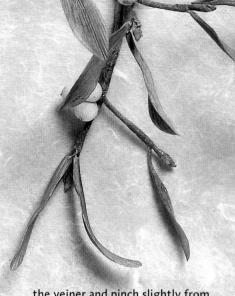

Berries

A touch of artistic licence is needed when producing the mistletoe fruit to give them a semi-translucent look.

1. Cut several short lengths of 30 or 33-gauge white wires. Burn the ends using the flame from a tea light or cigarette lighter to remove the paper and turn the wire black. Roll balls of white flower paste and insert a moistened wire into each. Press the ball of paste down against the burnt tip of the wire so that it shows through slightly. Allow to dry a little before dusting.

2. Dust the berries with some White Satin Bridal Satin Lustre Dust to give them a slightly translucent look. Catch areas of each berry lightly with a mixture of Vine and Edelweiss Dust Food Colours.

3. Carefully paint four dots around the protruding wire on the berry using either a Blackberry Food Colour Pen or a paintbrush and Blackberry Liquid Food Colour. (Do not worry if there are some dots missing here and there.) Allow to dry and then dip into confectioners' glaze.

Leaves

The leaves grow in pairs. They are quite thick and leathery in texture.

4. Roll out some pale Holly/Ivy coloured flower paste quite thickly, leaving a thicker ridge down the centre for the wire. Cut out the leaf shape using one of the three vanilla orchid outer petal cutters. Make several leaves in the same way using the three orchid cutters to give a little variation to the shape. To add a little more variation, cut out some leaves freehand using the plain-edge cutting wheel (or see templates on page 143).

5. Insert a moistened 30 or 28-gauge white wire into each leaf so that it is into about half the length of the ridge. Soften the edge of the leaf slightly using a metal ball tool. Place the leaf into the Stargazer B petal veiner to give it a soft, textural vein. Remove the leaf from

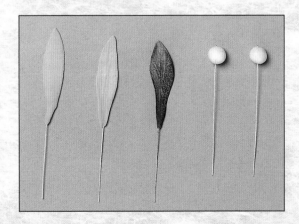

the veiner and pinch slightly from the base through to the tip. Repeat to make a pair of mirror image leaves. Leave to dry slightly before dusting them.

Colouring and Assembly

6. Dust each leaf lightly with Forest Green petal dust. Over-dust in layers with Leaf Green, Holly/Ivy and touches of Vine and Edelweiss Dust Food Colours. Dip each leaf into a quarter or half-strength confectioners' glaze or simply steam the foliage to remove the dusted appearance. The leaves are not particularly shiny, however you might prefer to use a higher strength glaze.

7. Create a bud end to use at the top of each stem by wrapping half-width Nile green tape several times around a hooked 28 or 26-gauge wire. Increase the bulk at the centre of the bud, encouraging it to form a slight point at the tip. Use a pair of fine, sharp scissors to make a cut on either side.

8. Tape a leaf onto either side of the taped bud. Join two leafy stems together, and add two or three berries where they join together.

Recipes

Very Fruity Fruitcake

This is no ordinary rich fruitcake. It is heavy on the fruit and flavour front. I have adapted it from a recipe from my friend Tombi Peck. Her version was adapted from her mother's friend Lynn Sinclair's recipe, and was first published in the cake decorating bible Finishing Touches in 1986. My version of the recipe has changed gradually from when I first made it. I am not a huge fan of currants so I leave them out – I have replaced them with dried figs and prunes. I recently made this cake for my Dad's 60th birthday. It cut well and tasted extremely good considering it was baked only the day before the event! This recipe will make a very deep 12 inch cake or three 8 inch round cakes. You will need to double the recipe for a three-tier cake, and I suggest you line an extra small tin or two just in case you have some left over!

Ingredients

1kg (2lb / 8 cups) raisins

1kg (2lb / 8 cups) sultanas

500g (1lb / 4 cups) dried figs, chopped

500g (1lb / 4 cups) dried prunes, chopped

250g (8oz / 2 cups) glacé cherries, halved

125g (4oz / 1 cup) glacé apricots, chopped

125g (4oz / 1 cup) glacé pineapple, chopped

Grated zest and juice of 1 orange

200ml (5floz / $^1/_2$ cup) Madeira, marsala wine, or brandy

500g (1lb / 2 cups) unsalted butter (at room temperature)

500g (1lb / 2 cups) light muscovado sugar

20ml (4tsp) apricot jam

40ml (8tsp) golden syrup

500g (1lb / 4 cups) plain (all purpose) flour

5ml (1tsp) each ground ginger, allspice, nutmeg, cloves and cinnamon

2.5ml ($^1/_2$ tsp) ground mace

250g (8oz / 1$^1/_2$ cups) ground almonds

10 large free range eggs (at room temperature)

Method

1. I use a large pair of kitchen scissors to halve and chop up the various fruit listed above. Add or subtract fruit accordingly to your taste. Mix the dried fruit, orange zest and juice and the alcohol together. Leave in a cool place to soak for about a week at best, otherwise overnight.

2. Cream the butter until soft. Gradually add the sugar and cream well. Stir in the jam and golden syrup and spices.

3. Sieve the flour into a separate bowl and stir in the ground almonds.

4. Beat the eggs together and add slowly and carefully to the butter mixture, alternating it with the flour/almond mix. Do not add the eggs too quickly or the mixture will curdle.

5. Set aside some of the mixture before you add the dried fruit to the remainder. This mixture is used on top of the fruited mixture in the tin to prevent burnt fruit on the top of the cake. Mix the fruit into the remaining larger amount of batter. Grease and line the tin(s) with non-stick parchment paper. Fill the prepared tin(s) to about two-thirds full. Apply a layer of un-fruited mixture on top. Bake in a preheated oven at 140°C (Gas Mark 1) for 4 – 6 hours, depending on the size of the tin. Keep a close eye on how the cakes are baking. When baked, the cake will shrink slightly away from the sides of the tin, it will have a lovely aroma, and it will feel firm to the touch. To check if the cake is cooked, insert a skewer into the centre. If it comes out clean, it is ready. If the cake is making a bubbling noise, it is not fully baked.

6. Allow the cake to cool in the tin before turning out and wrapping in non-stick parchment paper and cling film. Allow to mature at least overnight. It can be left for up to three months.

Flower Paste

The type of flower paste (gum paste) you use is a matter of personal preference. A paste that stretches well and does not dry out on the surface too quickly will allow you to wire and colour petals together while they are still damp. Ready-made flower paste, such as Squires Kitchen Sugar Florist Paste, tends to be more consistent than home-made paste and will save you a lot of time and hassle. However, if you wish to make your own, I would recommend the following recipe:

Ingredients

25ml (5tsp) cooled, boiled water

10ml (2tsp) powdered gelatine

500g (1lb / 4 cups) icing (confectioners') sugar

15ml (3tsp) gum tragacanth

10ml (2tsp) liquid glucose

10ml (2tsp) white vegetable fat (shortening)

1 medium egg white (preferably free range)* or equivalent amount of reconstituted, pasteurized, dried albumen powder

*IMPORTANT NOTE: The Foods Standards Agency recommends using only pastuerised egg in any food that will not be cooked (or will only be lightly cooked). If you decide to use fresh egg white, buy eggs with a 'Lion Mark' as they are guaranteed free from salmonella. Do not use damaged eggs. For more information and advice, contact the Foods Standards Agency.

Method

1. Mix the water and gelatine together in a small, heatproof bowl and leave to stand for 30 minutes. Sift and mix together the icing sugar and gum tragacanth into the bowl of a heavy-duty food mixer.

2. Place the bowl containing the gelatine mixture over a saucepan of hot water and stir until the gelatine has dissolved. Warm a teaspoon in hot water, then measure out the liquid glucose – the heat should help to ease the glucose off the spoon.

3. Add the glucose and white fat to the gelatine mixture and continue to heat until all of the ingredients have melted and are thoroughly mixed together. Add the dissolved gelatine mixture to the icing sugar, along with the egg white. Fit the 'K' beater to the machine and turn on at its lowest speed. Beat until mixed, and then increase the speed to maximum until the paste becomes white and stringy.

4. Remove the flower paste from the bowl and rub a thin layer of white fat over it to prevent the outer part from drying out. Place in a food-grade plastic bag, store in an airtight container and refrigerate. Allow the flower paste to rest and mature for at least 12 hours before using.

Working with Flower Paste

The paste should be well kneaded before you start to roll out or model a flower, otherwise it will start to dry out and crack around the edges. If the paste is dry or tough, soften it with fresh egg white (not gum arabic, etc.) – see Important Note*. If the paste is too sticky, add a small amount of white vegetable fat. Do not add too much as this will make the paste short and difficult to work, plus it will take longer to dry.

Always grease the board with white vegetable fat, then remove it almost completely with absorbent kitchen paper. This will form a very thin layer of fat and will stop the paste sticking to the board. Take care not to use too much fat as this will leave a layer on the surface of the petals that will show up in greasy patches when dusted.

Cornflour is used to dust the surface of the flower paste when rolling out or handling petals with hot, sticky hands. I always use fresh egg white to moisten wires for petals, leaves and sticking petals together. Fresh egg white dries faster and more efficiently than gum arabic, rose water and edible glues, which are favoured by some cake decorators. Always use eggs with a 'Lion Mark'; if you have any doubts about using fresh egg white, you may choose edible glue instead.

Flower paste is an air-drying paste so it is best to cover petals, leaves, etc. when you are not working on them with clingfilm, a food-grade plastic bag or a CelFlap (CelCakes).

Cold Porcelain

This is an allied craft, air-drying medium. However, the paste is completely inedible. The paste is much stronger than flower paste and is not as sticky as it contains no sugar. Flowers can be modelled in exactly the same way as sugar flowers. Once made, the flowers should be treated like fresh or silk flowers on a cake, i.e. they should not touch the surface of the cake or any item that is to be eaten (unless it is expressly stated by the manufacturer that it is safe to place on food). Flowers made from cold porcelain can be used in a vase, on a candleholder or displayed next to the cake.

There are several brands of ready-made cold porcelain available. However, if you wish to make your own, the following recipe is recommended:

Materials

37ml (2$\frac{1}{2}$ tbsp) baby oil

125ml (4fl oz/ $\frac{1}{2}$ cup) non-toxic, high-tack glue (Impex)

125ml (4fl oz/ $\frac{1}{2}$ cup) white PVA wood glue (Liberon Super wood glue)

125g (4 oz/ 1 cup) cornflour (cornstarch)

Permanent white gouache paint

IMPORTANT NOTE: Special care must be taken to work in a very well-ventilated area when making cold porcelain. Do not keep food in the same room whilst you are making the paste.

Method

1. Measure the baby oil into a medium-sized, non-stick pan and add the two glues. Stir them together to form an emulsion. Stir in the cornflour – you will find that it goes lumpy at this stage. Place the pan over a medium heat and stir until the paste has collected around the spoon (as for choux pastry). Scrape any uncooked paste from the spoon as you are cooking. The cooking time varies between gas, electric and ceramic hobs. Keep turning the paste to cook it evenly. You will need to split the ball of paste in order to cook it through.

2. Turn the paste onto a non-stick board and knead until smooth. If the paste is very sticky it is undercooked, so simply scrape it all up and reheat for a few minutes. It is better to have an undercooked batch rather than an overcooked one, which will be too tough to make flowers with. Wrap in clingfilm and allow to cool. When cool, re-knead and re-wrap the paste. Store in an airtight container at room temperature. The paste, if kept well, should last about a year.

3. Add permanent white gouache paint to the paste to prevent yellowing and extreme translucence. I tend to add the paint just before I am about to make flowers with it. Use cold face cream (e.g. Pond's or Boots' cream cleanser) instead of white fat as you would for sugar. Water and glue can be used to stick petals and cornflour is used in exactly the same way as for sugar. The paste shrinks as it dries, which can be a little difficult to get used to at first. However, this can be advantageous as it also results in slightly finer petals and leaves.

Royal Icing

Proprietary royal icing mixes and fortified albumen blends are commercially available, both of which contain pasteurised egg powder, thus eliminating the risk of salmonella contamination associated with raw eggs. Squires Kitchen Instant Mix Royal Icing is one such product and has the added advantage of being quick and convenient to use.

You can also make your own royal icing. This is the recipe I use when I only require small amount of royal icing for shells, snail trails and embroidery. I add a pinch of tartaric acid to the egg white before mixing if I am piping fine lace work. For extension work, add two drops of acetic acid instead. These are added to alter the PH balance of the egg white.

Ingredients

1 medium egg white (preferably free-range and at room temperature) – see above and Important Note on page 133*

225g (8oz/ 1$\frac{3}{4}$ cups) icing (confectioners') sugar, sifted

Method

1. Wash the mixer bowl and the beater with concentrated detergent and scald to remove any traces of grease or detergent. Place the egg white into the bowl and add the majority of the sieved icing sugar.

2. Fix the bowl and beater to the machine and beat on the slowest speed until it has reached full peak; this takes about eight minutes. You might need to mix in a little more sugar if it is too soft.

Equipment

Non-Stick Board and Rolling Pin

A non-stick board and small rolling pin are essential. A dark green board is preferable to a white board, which tends to strain the eyes as you are working. Grooved boards are also commercially available and can be useful. Alternatively, you can groove the back of your own board; heat a metal round skewer until it is red-hot. Brand a line on the back of the board. Repeat several times to achieve the depth of groove desired. Scrape off the excess plastic with a hot knife, or simply smooth over with fine glass paper or an emery board. A non-slip mat is also essential to place under the board while you are working to stop it sliding around.

Foam Pads

There are several food-grade foam pads available. They are used as an alternative to working on your palm and are particularly useful if you have hot hands. The petal or leaf can be placed on it and softened or veined. My favourite is a large blue pad called a Billy's block! I also use a yellow CelPad with holes in for some flowers. It is best to feel the material of the pad before you buy it – some have a fairly rough, open texture that easily tears the edges of petals.

Ceramic Silk Veining and Smooth Tools (Holly Products)

The silk veining tool has a series of veins on it and is great for creating a delicate, veined surface on petals and for frilling them. The smooth tool is also useful for opening up the centre of flowers and for curling the edges of rose petals. I also use the rounded end of both tools to hollow out orchid columns and small petals.

Metal Ball Tools

These are comfortable to handle and, being a little heavier in weight than plastic tools, they can be used to soften petals with minimum effort. To soften petals, place the ball tool half on the edge of the petal and half on your hand or a pad. I tend to use a rolling action to thin the edge of the paste, rather than the more traditional rubbing method.

CelSticks (CelCakes)

These are non-stick tools in four sizes: small, medium, large and extra large. The rounded end can be used to soften the edges of petals, and the other pointed end is useful for opening up the centre of flowers. They can also be used as mini rolling pins, especially for 'hat' shaped flowers and forming thick ridges for leaves and petals.

Dresden (Veining) Tool

This tool has a fine end and a larger, flatter end. The fine end is used for drawing lines on leaves and petals. The broad end can be used to draw veins and to hollow out the edges and centres of petals, sepals and leaves. It can also be used to create an effect commonly known as 'double frilling'. Simply press the tool repeatedly on the edge of a leaf or petal to create either a frilled or jagged/serrated edge – the effect depends on the angle at which the tool is applied to the paste.

Plain-Edge Cutting Wheel (PME)

This tool enables you to cut out sugar petals and leaves without any 'pulling' on the paste. A pizza wheel can also be good for cutting out larger objects.

Cutters and Templates

There is a huge selection and numerous brands of cutters available. Cutters speed up the process of shape cutting and help give consistency and accuracy to your work. Metal cutters come in a great variety of shapes and can be adjusted if necessary by bending with fine-nosed pliers. Plastic cutters are useful too, especially for intricate shaped foliage. Templates can also be used if cutters are not available or too expensive – however, they tend to slow down the flower making process. I often use templates when I am designing and making a flower for the first time. Colour photocopying or scanning the leaves or petals of a plant is an excellent and quick way of recording their exact shape, size and colour for your reference.

SK Great Impressions Veiners

These are double sided, food-grade silicone rubber veiners moulded from real flowers and foliage. They are extremely useful for adding realism to flower work. Once you have cut out the petal or leaf, inserted a wire and softened the edge, place the shape into the veiner. The ridge on the back of the paste should fit into the back of the veiner. Place the top section onto the petal and press down firmly.

Stamens

There is a vast array of ready-made, commercial stamens available to the flower maker. However, I tend to favour fine white and seed head stamens and colour them as required using food colour.

Wires

I use mainly paper-covered white wires, preferring to tape over or colour the wire green as I need it. The quality varies between brands – I prefer Sunrise Wires or the A-grade (identified by a red spot on the packet) from Hamilworth. Wires are generally available from 33-gauge (fine) to 24-gauge (thicker), and then there are very strong wires from 22-gauge to 14-gauge (the higher the number the finer the wire). There is also very fine, silk-covered 36-gauge wire on a reel which is ideal for tiny flowers.

Pliers, Wire Cutters and Scissors

Small, fine-nosed pliers are another essential item. They can be purchased from electrical supply shops. Wire cutters are also useful: you can use either electrical cutters or heavy-duty florists' scissors. I also use fine embroidery scissors, both straight and curved, for cutting petals and thread stamens.

Floristry Tape

This tape has a glue in it that is released when stretched, so it is important to stretch the tape firmly as you tape over a wire. I use mainly Nile green tape (Lion Brand). I also use white, beige, brown and twig coloured floristry tape.

Tape Shredder

This is wonderful sugarcraft gadget. It is used to cut full-width floristry tape into finer lengths. If you remove one of the three blades you will have a shredder that cuts one half and two quarter-width lengths of tape at the same time. The blades are actually razor blades and will need to be replaced regularly as the glue and paper from the floristry tape often builds up on them.

Non-Toxic Glue Stick and High-Tack Craft Glue

Non-toxic glue sticks can be bought from stationery shops and are used for fixing ribbons to cake boards. Always make sure that the glue does not come into contact with the cake covering. High-tack craft glue (Impex) is used to glue stamens onto wire. It should not come into contact in its wet state with sugar as it tends to dissolve it. Some sugarcrafters feel that inedible glue should not be used in the flower making process, however, as long as it is used carefully and the flowers are not intended to be eaten, I am happy to use it. There are many other inedible items used in the making of sugar flowers, such as wire, stamens, floristry tape and thread, so it is vital that the flowers are removed before the cake is eaten.

Florists' Staysoft

This is a form of soft modelling material sold in blocks by florists' suppliers, some cake decorating specialists and art shops. Arranging flowers into Staysoft allows them to be removed and rearranged easily if needed. A container or acrylic disc must be used underneath so that it does not come into direct contact with the cake.

Paintbrushes

Short, flat, firm synthetic brushes are best for applying dust colours to flowers and foliage. Good quality, synthetic mix brushes are available from sugarcraft suppliers such as Squires Kitchen, plus art suppliers including Robert Simmons ('Craft Painters' range) and Windsor and Newton ('Natural Grip' range). Numbers 6 and 8 are the two sizes I use most often for sugar flowers. A short, flat brush is also useful for colouring flowers accurately and efficiently. Sable brushes are another option, but they are expensive and tend to get damaged when used to rub dust food colour into petals and leaves.

You will also need some finer sable or synthetic blend brushes for painting finer detail. It is best to try to keep a different brush for each main colour to prevent the colours from mixing.

Thread

Fine, white, lace-making cotton thread (Brock 120) is best for stamens, although some thicker threads may also be useful. An emery board is also great for creating fluffy tipped stamens.

Posy Picks

Posy picks (or cake picks) are made from a food-grade plastic. They are used to hold the handle of a wired spray or bouquet to prevent the wires coming into direct contact with the cake. They are available in several sizes and are great for positioning flowers at odd angles into the cake. It is vital that wires are never inserted directly into a cake – always use a cake pick.

Smoothers

Sugarpaste smoothers are essential to create a smooth, polished finish to a sugarpaste coating. I use a round-edged smoother for the top surface of a cake and a flat-edged one to cut away the excess sugarpaste around the base of the cake. The latter is also useful for smoothing the sides to create a neat join between the cake and board.

Coating a Cake

Almond Paste (Marzipan)

For best results, always use a good quality white almond paste with a high almond content (minimum 23.5%) such as Squires Kitchen Marzipan.

1. Brush the cake with warm apricot glaze (thinned apricot jam purée). On a clean, dry surface, knead the almond paste to make it pliable. It is important that the surface is clean and free from flour or cornflour as these can become trapped between the almond paste and sugarpaste and potentially cause fermentation.

2. Lightly dust the work surface with icing sugar and roll out the paste to the approximate shape and size required to cover the cake. Smooth over the surface using a round-edged sugarpaste smoother.

3. Lift the paste over the cake and gently ease it onto the top and the sides of the cake. Use your hands to smooth the paste into place and then smooth over the top with a round-edged smoother. Use a flat-edged smoother to trim away the excess paste from around the base of the cake and to smooth the sides.

4. Place the cake on a sheet of greaseproof or parchment paper and into a cake box. Leave in a cool, dry place for a few days (or at least overnight) to dry before coating with sugarpaste.

Sugarpaste

Most cake decorators use a commercial, ready-made sugarpaste. There are several brands available; all the cakes in this book were coated with Regalice kindly supplied by Renshaw.

1. Knead the paste until smooth and pliable, avoiding the addition of air bubbles. Roll out on a board dusted with icing sugar. Smooth over the surface using a round-edged sugarpaste smoother. If there are any air bubbles visible at this stage, simply prick them with a fine glass-headed pin, and then quickly smooth over again with the smoother. Make sure you put the pin away safely.

2. Moisten the surface of the almond paste using a clean, food-grade sponge and some clear alcohol (spirit). I prefer to use cherry or orange liqueur as they taste and smell great. The alcohol acts as an anti-bacterial agent, but you might prefer to use a little cooled, boiled water instead. Try not to leave any dry patches on the almond paste as this can create areas where more air bubbles can be trapped.

3. Carefully lift the sugarpaste using the rolling pin and position it over the cake. Lift and smooth over the paste on top of the almond paste, trying to eliminate any air bubbles as you work. Smooth and trim the paste in the same way as for the almond paste. A pad of sugarpaste pressed into the palm of your hand can also be used to add further smoothness to the sugarpaste, and also to smooth out any hard to reach areas of difficult-shaped cakes.

4. If you are going to place the cake on a drum (board), brush it with clear alcohol, cover it with sugarpaste and smooth in the same way as for the cake. Trim away the excess paste from around the edge using a sharp knife in a downwards motion.

5. Position the cake on the covered cake board and once again use the straight-edged smoother to neaten and blend the join at the base of the cake where it meets the board.

Making Sugar Flowers

Wiring Petals and Leaves

There are many techniques for wiring petals: below is the method I use most frequently.

1. Roll out a piece of well-kneaded flower paste to the required thickness, leaving a thicker ridge down the centre – this can be achieved by rolling out the paste with a small rolling pin, manipulating the paste as you roll to leave a thick ridge for the wire. Alternatively, you may choose to roll the paste onto a grooved board to make the thick ridge needed for wire insertion.

2. Cut out the petal shape, positioning the ridge down the centre of the cutter. Press firmly down, and then release the paste from the cutter. Sometimes it helps if the paste is held in the cutter so that you can rub your thumb over the edge to release it and smooth over any rough edges left by the cutter.

3. Moisten the end of the wire with fresh egg white (see Important Note on page 133) or edible glue. Be careful not to use too much as this will make the petal too sticky and will also encourage the paper to come off the wire. Hold the ridge firmly between your finger and thumb, and hold the wire in the other hand very close to the end that you are inserting into the ridge. Push the wire into about a third to half the length of the petal or leaf to give support.

Glazing

There are several ways to glaze sugar flowers and foliage. The steaming method is used to create a 'waxy' finish or to set and remove the dry, dusted appearance left by dust food colour and craft dust. It can also be used to achieve a velvety finish or for darkening the depth of colour on a petal or leaf as the added moisture enables extra colour to be added. Hold each flower or leaf in the steam from a boiling kettle for a few seconds, or until the surface turns shiny. Check your work every few seconds as too much steam will dissolve the sugar. Always take care not to scald yourself on the steam.

For a more permanent and shiny glaze, use confectioners' glaze/varnish. Used neat as a full glaze it can be great for berries and glossy leaves. I generally dilute the glaze for most foliage to give a more natural shine. Use isopropyl alcohol to dilute the glaze (often sold in cake decorating shops as glaze cleaner or dipping solution). Mix the varnish and glaze together gently in a lidded container. Do not shake too vigorously as this will create too many air bubbles. I usually dip my leaves straight into the glaze, shaking off the excess and either hanging to dry or placing on absorbent kitchen paper. (The glaze may be painted on but I often find that this removes the dusted colour and causes streaks to appear.)

When making sugar flowers and leaves, I tend to use three different proportions of confectioners' glaze:

Three quarter-strength glaze: 1 part isopropyl alcohol to 3 parts confectioners' glaze. This gives a good glaze without creating the 'plastic' often left by full glaze.

Half-strength glaze: equal proportions of alcohol and varnish. This gives a good, natural shine for many types of foliage, especially ivy and rose leaves.

Quarter-strength glaze: 3 parts alcohol to only 1 part varnish. This is used for some petals and leaves that don't require much shine and it just takes away the flat, dusty look left by dust food colour and craft dust.

There are also food spray varnishes available. I use one by a company called Fabilo. It gives a good, even high glaze, ideal for glossy foliage, fruit and berries. Spraying leaves is much quicker than dipping them into confectioners' glaze.

Using a 'Cage'

A wire 'cage' is used to divide the surface of a bud to represent its unopened petals. To make a 'cage', tape together several wires at one end with some floristry tape. Bend it over again and re-tape to prevent the wires escaping during use. The gauge of wire will depend upon the size of bud, and the number of wires will depend on the number of petals of the flower you are making. Open up the cage and insert the modelled bud, tip or base first depending on the effect required. Close the 'cage' wires onto the bud, keeping them evenly spaced. Indent the wires into the paste to leave a mark. For some buds a more realistic effect may be achieved by pinching each of the petals through the cage to thin them down and make the petals more developed. Remove the bud from the cage and twist to give a spiralled, opening bud effect.

Colouring

Dust, Paste and Liquid Food Colours (Edible)

Food colours are available in three forms – paste, liquid and dust (sometimes referred to as 'powder' colours). Squires Kitchen's extensive range of colours is completely food approved for the European Union (legislation may vary in other parts of the world), so is recommended for use with cake coverings and decorations such as sugar flowers.

Dust food colours are available in a huge range. They can be used to colour flower paste, but should be limited to small amounts as they can alter the consistency of the paste, making it difficult to work with. They are, however, more commonly brushed onto sugar work once it has been made. It is important to have a good selection of dust food colours and to experiment with different colour combinations to achieve the effect required. The colours can be mixed together or brushed on in layers to create depth. If you want to make a colour paler, simply add some SK Edelweiss (white) Dust Food Colour. (Some sugarcrafters add cornflour, but I would not recommend this method as it lessens the gum content of the colour, thus making it adhere less to the paste.) By mixing isopropyl alcohol (SK Glaze Cleaner) with dust food colour, a quick-drying, edible paint is made which can also be applied to sugar decorations such as flowers and leaves. This is ideal for finer details such as spots or streaks.

Paste food colour can be kneaded into the sugarpaste or flower paste to create a basic colour. I use a small selection of paste food colours in both sugarpaste and flower paste. I prefer to make my flowers with a paler version of how I intend the flower to look, adding depth and further colour with dust colours at a later stage. To colour a large amount of sugarpaste (i.e. for covering a cake), knead some paste food colour into a small piece of paste and blend this into the remaining paste. This method makes it easier to blend in the paste colour. More colour can be added in the same way if required.

Liquid food colours are used to paint detail such as spots on petals and leaves. SK Cyclamen and Poinsettia Liquid Food Colours are particularly useful for the flowers in this book.

Craft Dust Colours

(Inedible)

These colours can only be used on items that are not intended to be eaten. As all of the flowers and leaves in this book are wired (and are made with other inedible items such as cotton thread and stamens), they are clearly not for consumption, so I have used a number of inedible craft dusts to create various colour effects. All craft dusts used in this way must be non-toxic and must not have direct contact with the cake, cake covering (sugarpaste), or any other item which is intended to be eaten. To avoid contamination, it is advisable to place any flowers, leaves, etc. with craft dust colourings away from the cake, or on a protective layer such as a clear, acrylic disc or a thin cake board. Any inedible dust colour used on these items should not have 'loose' dust that can be dislodged onto the cake or cake covering. Dust colours can be fixed by glazing the items, either by steaming them or dipping into confectioners' glaze (see page 138). It is vital that only colours that have been approved for food use are applied to edible items and coatings. Edible dust food colours and inedible craft dusts can be mixed together to create new colours, but the combination must be regarded as inedible.

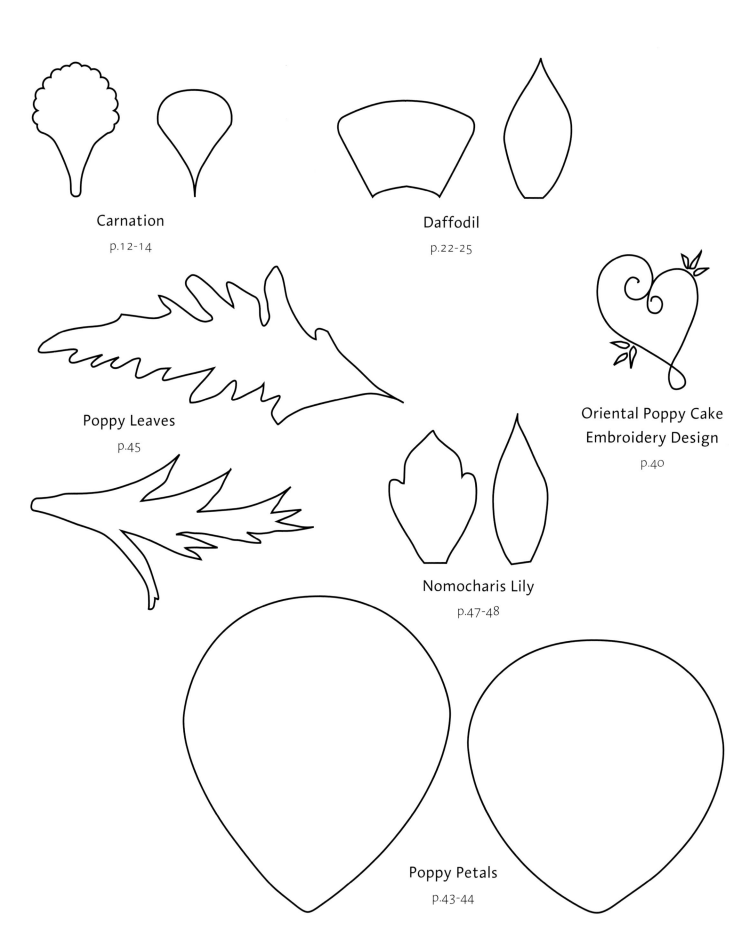

Carnation

p.12-14

Daffodil

p.22-25

Poppy Leaves

p.45

Oriental Poppy Cake
Embroidery Design

p.40

Nomocharis Lily

p.47-48

Poppy Petals

p.43-44

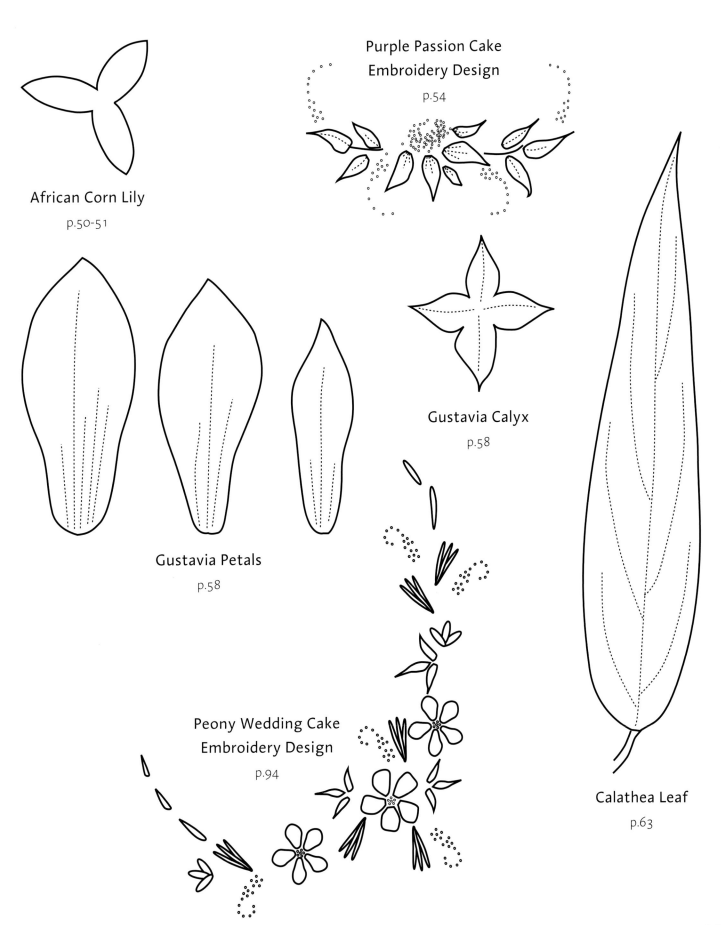

African Corn Lily

p.50-51

Purple Passion Cake
Embroidery Design

p.54

Gustavia Calyx

p.58

Gustavia Petals

p.58

Peony Wedding Cake
Embroidery Design

p.94

Calathea Leaf

p.63

Peony Petals p.97-98

Peony Calyx

p.98

Peony Leaves

p.99

Freesia

p.101

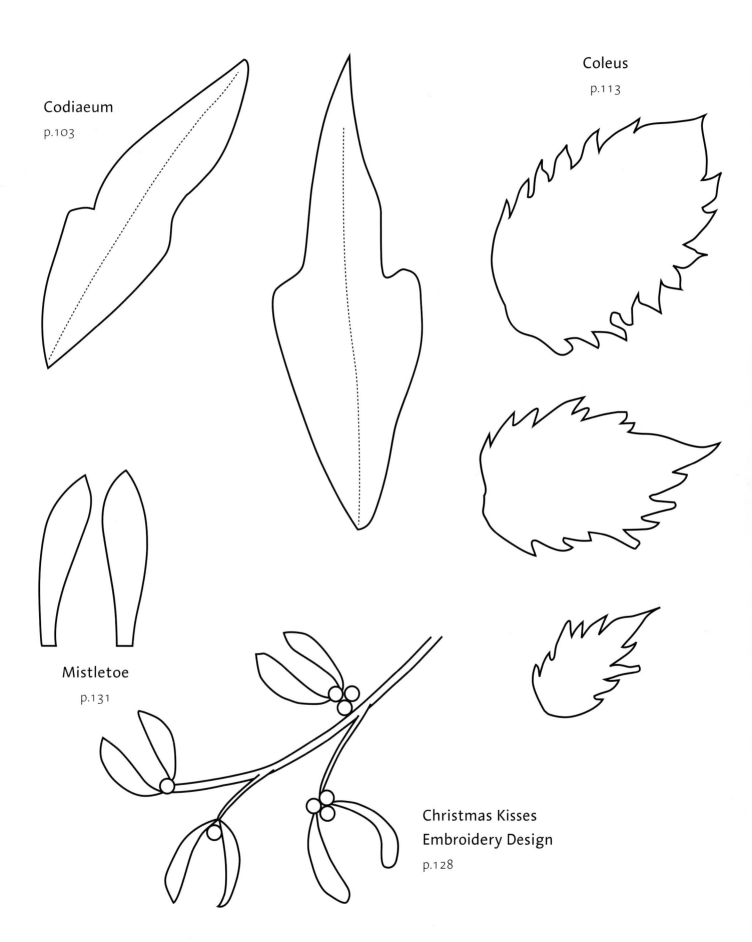

Codiaeum

p.103

Coleus

p.113

Mistletoe

p.131

Christmas Kisses
Embroidery Design

p.128

Suppliers

United Kingdom

Squires Kitchen (SK)

Squires House
3 Waverley Lane
Farnham
Surrey
GU9 8BB
Tel: 0845 22 55 67 1/2 (UK)
0044 1252 711 749 (Overseas)
Email: info@squires-group.co.uk
www.squires-group.co.uk
www.squires-shop.com

Supplier of SK Great Impressions range, sugarcraft colours, cocoa butter and other edibles, tools, equipment, marzipan and icings. Squires Kitchen is part of the Squires Group, publisher of sugarcraft books and magazines, school of cake decorating and sugarcraft, shop, online shop and mail order.

AP Cutters (AP)

Treelands
Hillside Road
Bleadon
Western-super-Mare
B24 OAA
Tel: 01934 812 787

A Piece of Cake

18 Upper High Street
Thame
Oxon
OX9 3EX
Tel/Fax: 01844 213 428
E-mail: Sales@sugaricing.com

Supplier of sugarcraft edibles, Sunrise Wires, fine lace makers' thread, silk-covered scientific wire, tools and equipment, including Fabilo spray varnish

Cakes, Classes and Cutters

23 Princes Road
Brunton Park
Gosforth
Newcastle-upon-Tyne
NE3 5TT
Tel/Fax: 0191 217 0538

CelCakes and CelCrafts (CC)

Springfield House
Gate Helmsley
York
YO4 1NF
Tel/Fax: 01759 371 447
www.celcrafts.co.uk

Confectionery Supplies

31 Lower Cathedral Road
Cardiff
Gwent
NP5 4BQ
Tel: 01600 740 448

Country Cutters (CCUT)

Lower Tresauldu
Dingestow
Monmouth
Gwent
NP5 4BQ
Tel: 01600 740 448

Culpitt Cake Art

Jubilee Industrial Estate
Ashington
Northumberland
NE63 8UQ
Tel: 01670 814 545

Framar Cutters (F)

19b Moor Road
Broadstone
Dorset
BH18 8AZ
Tel: 01202 659 760

Guy, Paul & Co. Ltd.

Unit 10, The Business Centre
Corinium Industrial Estate
Raans Road
Amersham
Bucks
HP6 6EB
Tel: 01494 432 121
Email: sales@guypaul.co.uk
www.guypaul.co.uk

Holly Products (HP)

Holly Cottage
Hassall Green
Cheshire
CW11 4YA
Tel/Fax: 01270 761 403

Orchard Products (OP)

51 Hallyburton Road
Hove
East Sussex
BN3 7GP
Tel: 01273 419 418

Renshaw

Crown Street
Liverpool
L8 7RF
Tel: 0870 870 6954
Email: info@renshaw-nbf.co.uk
www.renshaw-nbf.co.uk
Suppliers of Renshaw's Regalice sugarpaste.

W. Robertson

The Brambles
Ryton
Tyne and Wear
NE40 3AN
Tel: 0191 413 8144

Sugarflair

Brunel Road
Manor Trading Estate
Benfleet
Essex
SS7 4PS
Tel: 01268 752 891

The British Sugarcraft Guild

Wellington House
Messeter Place
Eltham
London
SE9 5DP
Tel: 0208 859 6943
www.bsg.org

The largest sugarcraft organisation in the world aimed at everyone interested in the craft/art form. There are no entry qualifications, only enthusiasm. Local branches all over the UK hold exhibitions, competitions and other events for sugarcrafters in each region.

The Old Bakery

Kingston St Mary
Taunton
Somerset
TA2 8HW
Tel: 01823 451 205

The Secret Garden (florists)

19 Clayton Road
Jesmond
Tyne and Wear
Tel: 0191 281 7753

Tinkertech Two (TT)

40 Langdon Road
Parkstone
Poole
Dorset
BH14 9EH
Tel: 01202 738 049

Overseas

ECG Supplies

844 North Crowley Road
Crowley
TX 76036, USA
Tel: 001 817 297 2240
www.europeancakegallery.US
Sugar art supplies in the USA.

International Sugar Art Collection

6060 McDonough Drive
Suite D, Norcross
GA 30093, USA
Tel: 001 770 453 9449

Other manufacturers featured in the book are: Hamilworth (HW), Jem Cutters (Jem), PME Sugarcraft (PME), Scientific Wire Company (SWC), Wilton (W)